The Fifth Element

SUNY series, Praxis: Theory in Action

Nancy A. Naples, editor

The Fifth Element

Social Justice Pedagogy through Spoken Word Poetry

Crystal Leigh Endsley

SUNY PRESS

Cover art by Bentrice Jusu

Published by State University of New York Press, Albany

Printed in the United States of America

For information, contact State University of New York Press, Albany, NY
www.sunypress.edu

Production, Diane Ganeles
Marketing, Anne M. Valentine

Library of Congress Cataloging-in-Publication Data

Endsley, Crystal Leigh.
The fifth element : social justice pedagogy through spoken word poetry / Crystal Leigh Endsley.
pages cm. — (SUNY series, praxis, theory in action)
Includes bibliographical references and index.
ISBN 978-1-4384-5985-1 (hc : alk. paper)—978-1-4384-5986-8 (pb : alk. paper)
ISBN 978-1-4384-5987-5 (e-book)
1. Performance poetry—Social aspects. 2. Poetry—Social aspects. 3. Poetry—Study and teaching. 4. Oral interpretation of poetry. 5. Social justice—Study and teaching. I. Title.

PN4151.E64 2016
808.5'45—dc23 2015014433

10 9 8 7 6 5 4 3 2 1

"Collective Energy, energy, all around, it can pick you UP and it can knock you down!" CE, this is for you. Toby, the Wizard, I thank you for demonstrating the definition of dedication—commitment to excellence, to vision. Read this book as a mirror, as the ultimate shout-out, a permanent tribute, a "thank you" that has been stirring inside ever since you took a chance on me with those posters for the Robe. You handcrafted a piece of the confidence that throbs within me now, and I summon that reflection of light on most days. I deeply appreciate you, and your legacy lives in everything I touch.

Tony, I still remember your grad school interview and our first open mic . . . and the baboons. My Starfish, you shine so bright, you stay so true—to yourself and to those you love. You teach me to be unapologetic and to own it. We've come a long way baby, and I celebrate you. There is so much more to come. #baeforlife here's to many more episodes of the Crystal and Tony show!

Carlos, you remain the most proficient writer I know. Your ill wordplay even in conversations, your mellow energy off stage, and the piercing lasers that you unleash onstage demonstrate such remarkable balance. That balance remains one of the qualities you have that I try always to locate in this chaos called life. I'm so proud of you.

Stacey, you were right, sis! "One of ya'll definitely got my lyrics!" What a privilege to share the stage in so many different ways with you—under the theater spotlight and then as a poet. Your boundless imagination pushes me to forsake comfort for the pursuit of freedom. You are a dreamer, and I love you for that.

Alyssa, the Songbird, the voice. So many adventures, sharing so many first experiences, and those conversations! May your horizons always be broad. I can't wait to see how your harvest from the seed you've sown comes back to you. You don't even need a beat, mama, you can sing this a cappella.

Jonathan, Ol' Silky himself. Whether finessing the dance floor or letting those vocals loose, you have always done exactly what you wanted to do. Your determination to carve your own way artistically, academically, and even in the daily decisions of life, is something you do with such style. I cannot wait to see what else is in store for you.

Q'tyashia, we have truly come full circle. From the classroom to the stage to our road trips near and far, I am thankful for you sis. Your ability to see in me what I even hide from myself keeps me accountable and lets me know I can always turn to you. I can always come home. You are brave, a woman of actions, never afraid to take a chance. Watch ya step now.

For those reading this trying to find your way, living life in the "in-between" and uncertain about who you are, this is for you. For the artist, full of fire and the scholar who wants to just read, this is for you. For whatever reason you have picked up this book—you're holding a living dream in your hands. I wrote these stories in part to restore my own faith in spoken word—if God spoke the entire universe into existence with *words*, then surely they are brimming with creative energy when we use them; surely they are powerful when we speak them. Indeed, our words shape our lives. Let's give a whole new meaning to watching your mouth.

Contents

Contents

Acknowledgments

A version of chapter 3 was originally printed in J. Wallin, ed., *Democratizing Educational Experience: Envisioning, Embodying, Enacting*, © 2008 by Educator's International Press. Reprinted by permission of Educator's International Press. Used with permission.

Special thanks to the Office for Advanced Research at John Jay College for funding part of this project.

"Nothing But The Water (I)," words and music by Grace Potter, Matthew Burr, Scott Tournet and Bryan Dondero © 2006 Seven Peaks Music, Hobbitville Music, 5 Cent Checks, Illusion Tournet Music and Shakey, Underwood Music; all rights for Hobbitville Music, 5 Cent Checks, and Illusion Tournet Music administered by Seven Peaks Music, all rights reserved. Used by permission, reprinted by permission of Hal Leonard Corporation.

Cover art "The Fifth" is designed by Bentrice Jusu, inspired by Kayla Lee. Jusu is founder of Both Hands the Artlet and an award-winning interdisciplinary artist, filmmaker, and activist. Jusu currently serves as the advanced civic engagement liaison at The College of New Jersey and sits on the advisory council of the annual Trenton African American Cultural Pride Festival. Find her work at www.Bentrice.com.

Octavia Butler teaches us, "All that you touch you change. All that you change, changes you." I offer deep gratitude to those who were unafraid to be touched and were willing to do the work of changing me. To the departments of Curriculum and Instruction and Women's Studies, as well as the Paul Robeson Cultural Center at the Pennsylvania State University, for the resources and the support both of these environments provided me, I am grateful. To my guides, Drs. Patrick Shannon, Stephanie Springgay, Peggy Lorah, Miss Kathleen, Jacqueline Edmondson: for your sharp eyes, sharp wit, time, and energy I thank you. Mr. Charles and Miss Jo Dumas: for your timing and your spirit and your vision, I thank you. Dr. E (Elaine Richardson): for your example and your faith and for going the extra mile for me, I thank you. Dr. Cathy Lyons, because of your consistency in your support of me, then and now. Especially to Dr. Marnina Gonick: for never, ever giving up on me, for showing me that there is more than one way to win, that habit is more dependable than inspiration, and that Paris really is a dream come true, and for making room for this misfit at your table. So much love and gratitude.

Many thanks to Beth Bouloukos for your help and patience with me and this project, and to Diane Ganeles and Anne Valentine and the staff of State University of New York Press for all of their support.

To the poets and photographers and singers and musicians of the 757 who endlessly inspire me. From day one you've had my back and you've pushed my art. Neleh, Hamza, Marco Mercado, Rina and the Parrilla clan, Stef Love, J Pharoah and all of JMP crew, Kaveen, godchild, 13, Dan Tres: each of you have had such an impact on me, and I love ya'll. Thanks for passing the mic. To Droopy the Brokeballer for opening your home and your venue for my first out-of-town feature. Shout out to the rest of the original 5th Element poetry crew, who were the first to demonstrate to me what poetic collaboration could look like. To Dwayne Morgan, for wise counsel, for persistent loyalty, and for being a true friend onstage and when the spotlight fades. To Ingrid B of B Side Entertainment, Miami, Florida, for taking a chance on me way back, for showing me how it could be done proper. To Shaggy Flores, who booked my first college gig and who told me from day one that I had to publish. I am thankful for you reaching out into the dark to show me to the light. For all the stages and places and those who have given me refuge while I've been on the road.

To those pioneers, the brave mothers, teachers, strangers, working women, Sunday School teachers, musicians, and scholars who persisted, who carved out pathways, whose ideas wrapped me up when I was seeking comfort in the one place I've always found it—books. It is to your drumbeat that I move. I am grateful and I acknowledge your life and your work, because your example provided me with tools to survive. To Sister Inease, to Sister Ruth Lupton, and all of the ushers who remember my name, hug my neck, who pray for me on my travels, who write me letters, who encourage me, who love me enough to correct me, who supported my mama, and thus supported me. Your sacrifice was never in vain. To my first-generation academics, to the mixed kids, to the misfits, you're my kindred, may this book strengthen your spirits. To all the students who have shared lessons with me, making the world our classroom. Especially to the Feminists of Color Collective at Hamilton College and Bryn Mawr's Mujeres and the Women and Gender Studies and Africana Studies departments at George Mason University. You can do everything. All of it. Don't let anyone tell you different. To Noelle for being a friend and for having such style! while on the Hill.

To my "tear a hole in the roof" friends/folks/family. When I wanted to quit, when I was a hot mess, and when I was hungry you prayed and carried me through. You ain't never scared to let loose celebrating me, either. Erin Wyble Newcomb, your attention to this manuscript, our conversations, and your inclusion of me in your life is a cherished gift—neither I nor this book would be where we are without you. Harriet Huell Lampkin, for always making time for me. LeTrez Myer Cole, forever my family, my tribal council for always having my back. Erika Ospina Awad, for your consistency and for the chair that this book was written in! Nova, from day one you were always ready to expand the vision. Marla Lou, for the constant reminder that we are not meant to blend, and for opening doors. Angelito Nieves, for never compromising, for giving me a chance, for setting a standard. Lorenzo Baber, for getting it even when I couldn't say it out loud. Jenna Rae Jackson Murdock, for always making room for me. Shana Spearman, always in my corner, that's why you're the champ. Bruce Wayne Taylor, my only exception, for being steadfast, for your patience with me. Joseph Lyttle, for your loyalty, for telling the truth, for knowing me and loving me still. You are always the James Baldwin to my Lorraine.

I am thankful to my daddy, Michael Lee, and my mama, Clara Jean, for being such good archers, thrusting me into places you have never been, trusting God with me enough to let me go, and for always letting me come home. I appreciate each day the legacy of faith you have woven into our family, for your uncompromising integrity, for showing me that love is a verb, how to forgive, and how to set fire. My big brother Michael, I admire and respect you so much. I will always be trying to be as smart as you; Bubba—you are a man full of purpose, full of destiny. Thank you for never letting me take myself too seriously. The best is yet to come. For Malik Samuel and Ramiro Manuel, I am so proud of you. I love you and I appreciate the joy you bring. You challenge me to be better.

To my Creator, I honor you through and with this creation. You are the Author, and it has always really just been you and me. I choose to speak life. Ashe, ashe, and amen.

Prologue

Know thy self, and thou shalt know
The universe and God . . .

—KRS One, "Know Thy Self"

Jump

Crystal Leigh

No, ain't nobody worrying
Ain't nobody worrying about the girl who can't move one more foot in front of the other and is wondering if she
If she steps to the left
If she turns to the left if she leans to the left there is danger, even though it's hard to make out in the dark, the dark silhouette of danger waiting for her to move just the slightest bit to the left
Waiting for her to give the smallest inch of space
Because that's all fear needs to shoot its roots to the core of her soul to the core of the soles of her feet and her lean to the left, her step to the left will turn into a fall.

And this is for the girl who is wondering if she were to step to the right
If she were to turn to the right
Would that count as compromise, would her right turn translate to the turning of her back on what she faced
Would she be turning her back on them
Turning her back on
Trying to figure out how to turn her on, turn her back on
Without giving up her position without moving without breathing
Would the momentum it took to turn to the right swell into the crescendo that made her fall. Fall out of love fall down fall off the face of the world. Turning to the right doesn't make it the right thing to do.

Ain't nobody worrying
Because nobody sees
The sweat starting to bead around her hairline and trickle down the ditch in the middle of her back
Nobody looks long or hard enough to notice the tightness of her smile
Because she can smile and at the same time not move her feet.
She can smile and stand still.
To fall or to stay still, which is worse?
Which is worse?

Every nerve in her body is stiff
Rigid with adrenalin
Waiting
The only thing that's moving are her thoughts, her thoughts are racing, the next and newest thought eating the last one
But you would never know it.

Yes, her back is to the wall
And she remembers her mother's name.
But ain't nobody worrying
Nobody is thinking about the tightrope, the string that she walks on not quite sure
How she got on top, how the rope she was weaving got stretched tight enough to pop
When she decided to start walking, to use the tight rope to bridge her gap
And now she is in the middle
Again
and wondering
Should she turn to the left, should she move to the right,
or should she stand in the middle.
And the church judges
And the elders cluck
And the children watch
And the teachers grade
And the heads shake
And the hands grab
And she stands.
But nobody is the wiser

Should she stand or should she move or should she jump . . .
She jumped.

It's just another open mic night, and the featured performer has roughly twenty minutes to rock alongside her crowd. Bright spotlights catch floating specks of dust, glasses clink against wooden tables, and the air is warm because of the small venue. Warm tones of brown and black faces, with a few white ones standing out, make up the attendees. Age doesn't appear to be a prerequisite either, since there are a couple of folks with young children and some white-haired elders taking seats as well. A limited number of chairs forces much of the crowd to take a seat on the floor, right beside the stage, where the spotlight makes them glitter like sand. Others stand with elbows on the bar, leaning, eyes grazing the seated crowd with attention equal to what they give the poet on stage. So much of the vibe rides on the hosts: Do they joke with the attendees with such familiarity that it's easy to see they are regulars? Are they eccentric and cool, or do they cut up and dance during the musical interludes in between poets? The next poet is a virgin to the mic, and she walks up with a creased sheet of notebook paper in her hand. Because she's shaking, she has to unfold her poem and hold it with two hands. She begins to read. To her shock, they clap when she's finished, and she quickly mutters a "thank-you" and walks off the stage. Sweat collects in the ditch in the middle of her back, and though she's greeted with handshakes and hugs of congratulations on a job well done, she burns with embarrassment. One last girl comes up to hug her neck, and this girl isn't quite a friend but she is not unfamiliar. After the obligatory three seconds of hug, the new poet tries to step back to make her way to her seat. That's when the realization hit her—the girl was crying. Immediately distracted from her own discomfort, the poet wraps the girl in a firmer hug than before, as if it were the most natural thing in the world. Tears begin to soak into the new poet's collar, and she responds as if the girl were a child that needed consoling. "It's okay, it's alright," the poet whispers softly, trying not to draw attention to what's happening, glad for the privacy the darkness of the place affords.

"It felt like you were talking about me up there. It felt like you were talking about me," said the girl hoarsely.

And so it begins.

Spoken word poetry began much like hip hop and most other modes of cultural production—as an underground method of creative expression and social resistance—and has since become a trending practice from classrooms to commercials. My career as a spoken word poet began while I was an undergraduate in college and continued to grow through graduate school; I never dreamed my artistic endeavors would one day combine with scholarly pursuits. It was difficult and frustrating to piece together the sources of scholars who were doing work "like" mine, while their writings were not necessarily relating the most important themes (identity, performance, feminist pedagogy, activism) directly to the rehearsal and practice of spoken word poetry. My current performance work broadly engages with concepts of identity and performance as a form of pedagogy: the teaching and learning that occurs in moments of performance. Specifically, I ask what knowledge is constructed and acknowledged as valuable during these moments. How does spoken word poetry function as a form of pedagogy and what does it teach us? My work, indeed my very life, has always been interdisciplinary—although I have attempted and failed many times to separate personal from political (one racialized experience from another in my ambiguous body) and to distance my scholarship from my artistic performance and practice, it is impossible to do so. Although there are moments when I may privilege one identity over the others depending on my circumstance, I may simultaneously be discriminated against because of another aspect of my identities (see Crenshaw 1989; hooks 2000). I cannot be only my race(s) or only a gender or only a scholar or only a poet at any given time, nor do I wish to be. I decided that it was more worthwhile to examine these points of contact and conflict because the lives we lead are full of intersections, not only between ourselves and others but also among our own subjectivities. Spoken word poetry performance first provided me with an outlet, a vehicle, a tool, a space to sort through the contradictions of my lived experience. How to be both a woman and an academic? How to love and live for my home community and yet succeed in the academy without betraying that same home? How to be multiracial, the oppressed and the oppressor at any given moment, and yet work for social justice? How to be a survivor of rape and abuse and be a liberated and independent whole woman? How to be an activist and an artist and feminist and a scholar and a popular culture practitioner? How to claim equality and exercise power? How to be angry and yet forgive?

From this point of turmoil I found spoken word poetry. From graduate school I found feminist theory. This book braids my experience of working to engage fully and honestly with both of these worlds while also seeking success as an academic and an artist. My intention for this work is to position spoken word poetry, identity, and embodied performance as tools for socially responsible cultural production and activism in the lives of college students who are also emerging artists. As a scholar and an artist, I work to address the multiplicity of experiences of this integrated performing arts group on a college campus and abroad. The goal of this text is to explore spoken word poetry and performance as a tool for social justice, for critical feminist pedagogy, and as an element that is crucial to developing new ways of teaching and learning about identity.

The Fifth Element

The title of this text is reference and tribute to several cultural products that contribute to the performance of spoken word poetry and the community served by socially responsible art. The rowdy "cousin" of spoken word poetry, hip hop, is based on the premise that there are four fundamental elements: the DJ, Bboys/girls, graffiti, and the MC or lyricist. These elements are crucial to understanding the birth, purpose, and evolution of hip hop as a culture and as an art form. In the hip hop community, "the fifth element" is often unofficially recognized as the knowledge of self. Referring to the knowledge of self as the title of this work pays homage to the lineage of hip hop that spoken word poetry is undoubtedly connected to while asserting that there is another element that manifests itself and contributes to the development of self-knowledge: the performance of spoken word poetry. Finally, the title draws another component into the spotlight, one that is central throughout hip hop culture as well as in spoken word poetry: knowledge of self as social responsibility.

Hip hop and spoken word poetry are clearly related; they both prominently feature roots in resisting oppression, both are organic to communities of color, and both have a broad appeal for and accessibility to young people (see Dyson 2011; Neal and Forman 2004; Rose 1994). However, I have observed that there are clear distinctions in their practice as well as singular components that suggest the need to investigate spoken word poetry as a divergent art form with particular results. This comparison isn't intended to privilege one art form over the other but to distinguish their connections and differences in an effort to delineate what each practice has to offer (Eleveld 2005; Low 2011). First, hip hop encompasses a culture and a lifestyle, and the term is used as an umbrella for many manifestations of culture. From style of dress to manner of speech, hip hop influences and infiltrates a broad spectrum of behaviors. Meanwhile, spoken word poetry is just that: a specific performance technique that is a cultural product and not always or necessarily a culture. There's no particular fashion or look that might outwardly identify a spoken word artist. Most often confused with the hip hop element of the MC or lyricist, spoken word poetry is usually performed a cappella, whereas the MC typically relies on a beat or music to rhyme to. Spoken word poetry doesn't necessarily rhyme, though it often does, and hip hop lyrics must rhyme in order to function properly within the schema of their musical category. While content and delivery style are wildly diverse for both spoken word artists and MCs, the most striking difference between the two is *objective.* Regardless of the poem or song's theme, the objective of the performer marks the key point of departure for spoken word poets. An objective is the goal or aim for a particular performance piece: What does the artist hope to achieve through the performance? What is the key outcome the artist desires for the performance? Objective will determine delivery style, passion and intensity, word emphasis, and rhythm, and the objective of the performer belies that artist's goal. Equally important to the analysis undergone here, the objective of the spoken word artist determines the tactics used to achieve that goal during a performance. If my objective for a particular performance is to raise the stakes for my audience around a social issue such as domestic abuse, then I might perform using techniques that provoke empathy from my audience. This performance choice, rather than an angry or accusatory delivery style or tone of voice, may cause my audience to align their own emotional investment alongside that of my poem. Understanding the goal and objective of the artist is essential to embarking on a critical analysis of spoken word poetry and performance as a means of activism. As a fan, a student, a child of the hip hop generation, I believe strongly in hip hop as a tool for mobilization and activism as well, and there are a multitude of excellent sources and books that have extended those scholarly conversations (see Brown and Kwakye 2012; Collins 2006; Kitwana 2002; Morgan 2000; Porfilio 2010, Pough 2004). However, it's important to address the overlaps in practice and audience for hip hop and spoken word poetry because they are often lumped together, even though each provides specific spaces for the creative and energetic pursuit of social justice. Both spoken word poetry and hip hop are rooted in competition—to be the best, and therefore most respected, MC or poet; both have been quickly commodified, capitalized, packaged and marketed to the Western mainstream, and both are globalized. It is also important to note that spoken word and hip hop are not necessarily exclusive of one another—it is possible to do both and they often cross-pollinate, providing a richer aesthetic and deeper creative possibilities. My project here is to hone in on the specific ways that college students who are also emerging artists might develop their skills as spoken word artists toward an objective of service, of negotiating meaning, and reimagining their identities in new ways while reverencing and acknowledging the deep influence of hip hop scholarship that shapes my analysis.

Spoken word poetry also diverges a great deal from the traditional poetry reading we are often introduced to in a dry classroom setting. As with hip hop, there are characteristics that these two forms share, such as reliance on metaphor or simile, a pattern and rhythm. Even the initial appeal of writing creatively in an autobiographical approach or at an abstract angle remains the same. Spoken word performance and written poetry both "serve as a medium to speak about experiences in ways often not censored by structures and rules" (Jocson 2005, 132). There is a sense of liberation that exists and often lends the pleasure of release to the writer and reader of either spoken word or written poetry. However, the key difference is in the method of delivery: spoken word poetry is often presented as a performance, while poetry on the page is often read silently. Spoken word poetry demands that more than one of the five senses be engaged during a performance, and a poetry reading does not necessarily ask the same from an audience member. Typically, crowds that attend open mic nights are verbal in their reactions during a spoken word artist's time on stage, bearing witness by clapping, snapping, or vocalizing agreement in the midst of the performance, so it is not uncommon to also engage the sense of touch. The live performance is a physical experience that breaches the boundary of typical theatrical performances and wrests one-sided power away from the reader of a poetry book. Both forms involve "ones' ability to read, create, analyze and criticize," but spoken word poetry performance places the emphasis on relationship between the audience member and the artist, thus commanding an awareness of others as well as an increased awareness of the self as critical (Jocson 2005, 133). June Jordan's (1995) groundbreaking work also suggests that poetry serves as a central tool as an element of social change (Jocson 2005, 135). Because of spoken word poetry's reliance on the body and voice as mechanisms for sharing the work of the poet, this sort of performance offers a visceral experience that is difficult to ignore or compartmentalize even after the conclusion of a performance. Spoken word performances make audiences aware of the intersections inhabited by the artist because multiple senses are used to consume and engage with the work. Poetry that lives on the page does not require the same sort of analysis and digestion since the body of the artist is not necessarily called into play through a reading by the audience. Spoken word poetry solicits an embodied literacy and method of reading: bodies and voices instead of letters or text. Often shared in front of an audience made up of strangers and friends, in venues that vary from bars and lounges to auditoriums or street corners, spoken word poetry is a genre that does not require any specific external equipment. While a microphone and speakers are nice, they are not necessary—and this accessibility broadens the potential for social transformation.

History

In recent years, the art of spoken word poetry has gained recognition as a performance art with a wide following. Media productions such as the HBO series *Def Poetry Jam* offer mainstream exposure to lesser-known and recognized up-and-coming poets from across the United States while simultaneously providing a broad audience with an introduction to what was previously considered an underground art form (Bynoe 2004; Denzin 2003; Simmons 2004). Open mic venues have sprung up across the United States and internationally, hosting featured artists, self-publishing poets, and poetry slam competitions where regional slam teams comprised of poets battle for championship titles, monetary prizes, and bragging rights. Often highly political, the performances by rising poets and celebrities featured in such shows have been well documented and are easily accessible around the globe through DVD collections and YouTube videos. These are useful resources and prove helpful in exposing new audiences to this form of performance. The more recent *Brave New Voices* series tracked youth slam teams, made up of high school students, who competed against their peers for similar accolades (Simmons 2010). Riding the currents of interest and the legitimation of spoken word poetry and performance are a multitude of academic publications addressing the uses of spoken word poetry, from anthologies featuring prominent performers to "how-to" reference books designed to assist in teaching core curriculums such as social studies, English, and science using the method of performance poetry in secondary school classrooms (Eleveld 2005; Harper 2000; Smith 2006). There is a body of recent research that highlights the potentially powerful moments of teaching that can occur when critical pedagogy is purposefully infused with arts of all dimensions within a traditional classroom setting (Denzin 2003; Felman 2001; Giroux 2006; Simon 1992). While this literature is helpful as a teaching tool and highly productive when implemented as part of a curriculum, it does not account for the transformative ways that spoken word poetry, with content sharply focused on social change, might impact and shape the constructions of meanings and the transgressive relationships between audience and artists that are forged during a spoken word performance. Becoming a literate audience member requires a new understanding of power and the skill to read how certain bodies and histories are privileged over others.

I hope to use this text to boldly explore the raw, lived reality in a landscape of liminal space that exists between the stage and the lectern for audiences and artists who are also scholars. The practices of hip hop and spoken word poetry are powerful traditions that make social issues accessible, changeable, and dialogical to those most vulnerable among us. As a communicative tool and as a large vehicle for the diverse lived experiences of people of color often told by people of color, spoken word poetry has created space to project and rehearse multiple representations and signifiers. Meanwhile, feminist theory and poststructuralist thought both lend themselves to an analysis of the content and craft of spoken word poetry because of their emphasis on embodied performance. Judith Butler (1993) effectively clarifies the ways in which dominant discourses of patriarchy and racism determine how bodies are interacted with. She also suggests that we are able to revise these discourses because they are historical—in other words, as we perform our identities, we may also alter these oppressive structures Patricia Hill Collins (1991) names "the matrix of oppression." Performance opens doors to subvert or explicitly challenge the structures that bind and punish those of us who are marginalized, thus utilizing spoken word poetry as a tool of effective resistance. The layered meanings that constantly vie for the audience members' attention are too many to be taken up in a singular fashion. Instead, poststructuralist theory suggests that multiple meanings are possible and present in any one performance event (Boal 1979; Weedon 1997). As multiple meanings are negotiated and validated during the exchanges that occur in each performance, it makes sense to explore the possibilities spoken word poetry might offer toward activism through a feminist reading.

My initial approach to the material pulls from the purview of my experience as an internationally acclaimed spoken word artist who is also pursuing an academic career. Once on the university campus, I cofounded a team that began creating opportunities to perform at a predominantly White institution whose campus climate constantly shifted from hostile to comfortable—all while pursuing a doctorate, teaching, and working full-time on campus. Based on instances that emerged during the formation of a student artist performance group known as Collective Energy, this analysis aims to reconcile the often racist and clashing academic theory I learned in the classroom and my lived experiences working for the first time with student artists. On a deeper level, limited attention has been paid to the pedagogical encounters that occur when a spoken word artist enters the academy and engages as a member of the higher education community. I foreground this project by asking the following questions: How does spoken word poetry function as a tool for social change? What differences emerge during performances that take place in an open mic venue versus those that are produced within a classroom setting on a campus? How are these same performances transformed when enacted in an international setting? What can be learned from the experience of a scholar artist and student artist, and why is this process important?

Stage Directions

Toward a response to those questions, chapter 1 begins by establishing the context and theoretical framework for the integrated performing arts group that served as the research site and creative space this text is based on. This chapter lays a foundation using performance pedagogy theory, feminist theory, and arts-based inquiry as a starting point for further exploration. Next, I introduce the student artists who participated in Collective Energy and situate them in the roles that they initially played in the performance group. I pull support and examples from interview excerpts and lyrics from work created during Collective Energy workshops and performances.

Chapter 2 segues into my perspective as an artist and scholar, starting with an introduction to the various roles I took up during Collective Energy's formation, namely, that of "researcher" and that of "artist." In this chapter, I explore how these conflicting positions shaped my interactions with the "research(ed)" who were also my peers, colleagues, and students. I preface this chapter with a reference to these two roles in order to acquaint the reader with an idea of what it was like for me to slide and glide between different performances of my own off the stage. I also examine how spoken word poetry and performance function as a means of navigating and constructing the world.

In chapter 3, I situate a broad understanding of activism and approach that understanding from two angles: first, as it relates to the spoken word performances of Collective Energy. This chapter considers the ways in which performance functioned for members of Collective Energy as a means of reproducing their experiences in the world, thus resisting and changing them. Next, I intertwine the student artists' perceptions of activism with the responses and reactions I received after inviting students from a class I taught to attend a cultural program entitled Bed: A Spoken Word Lounge. I connect the inner workings of this small, integrated arts group to the larger context in which they carried out a majority of their daily activity in order to analyze the ways that spoken word poetry and performance functioned in our lives on an individual and relational level within our community.

The fourth chapter focuses upon a discussion of love and ethics and the ways my own performance served me in teaching and especially learning about the practice of both. I posit that although the relationship between love and ethics is not always recognized, both elements are always present in the discourse about one or the other. The necessarily cooperative existence of love and ethics provide an interesting and, for me, useful opening through which I can translate the experiences I have had as a leader and performer within Collective Energy. I suggest that it might also be helpful to make love and ethics the grounding and central motivation behind other theoretical and activist work that takes place within and beyond the academy.

The concept and performance art of spoken word poetry, like many genres of American music, pulls heavily on an African aesthetic and sensibility. So, in the final chapter, I address an arena that has not been written about extensively before: What happens when this art form, developed and used as a tool for activism in the United States, travels to the Caribbean, to East Africa, and then boomerangs back again? Here I explore the international and, specifically, the East African context for performing spoken word poetry, looking ahead to future possibilities for creating change and powerful performance art in a global context.

1

Mic Check

I want to clarify that this integrated performing arts group did not begin as a research project, only as a cultural program. It wasn't until we were deep into the detailed planning stages that I realized that implementing a training/workshop/sharing time with a group of young artists was a desire I'd had for a long time. Acknowledging this desire was for me a moment of lucidity. Transitioning from a performance poet to a mentor shifted how I viewed my own performances and my own purpose. Up to this point, my only goal was to be a dope artist and to get my degree. When I cofounded the group, my purpose became intertwined with the success of the student artists on and off stage. My goals stretched laterally because my energy was no longer flowing in only a vertical direction: from God, to me, to an audience. Instead my purpose widened to include teaching and learning with a group. Working in community was new and very powerful for me. So much of my experience as an artist and as an academic, the act of writing especially, takes place alone, in solitude. Concentration, competition, and discipline were taught to me as necessary for professional successes. Outsiders could not be trusted, so these successes were also individualistic endeavors. Plus, I had no "teachers" to look to while I was learning the ropes as a first-generation college student. I had to actively seek and pursue mentorships and friendships and endure the rejection of those that were refused. Community on campus was there, but not always obvious or even welcoming. But teaching and learning require an acknowledgment of the dependency we have on relationships with others. It was working with Collective Energy that taught this lesson to me. In performance, in spoken word poetry, and teaching in a classroom issues of objectives arise. Identifying the objective behind a decision or performance choice can help sharpen the precision and focus behind each subsequent action that is taken. The objective in this chapter is to clarify the overlapping goals and roles of two defining aspects of the Collective Energy experience: my own position as researcher and artist and the impact of spoken word poetry performance on the student artists.

As the cultural program continued, I realized that there wasn't much background written on a group like ours that was specifically geared toward spoken word poetry. There were many manuals and guidelines for general arts groups or for "poets," but most of these templates were focused on very specific demographics, and I constructed this group intentionally to avoid being generalized. They are not all students of color, they do not all identify as feminists, nor are they all first-generation college students.

My purpose behind this mixture of distinct experiences was precisely that: to bring these different elements together and see what happened. I feel that the wild variety in each component is what makes this project so important. Frequently, there are examples of research that focus on one particular ethnic group or socioeconomic status, but I have yet to find substantial work that focuses on such a varied community of people who, instead of sharing a particular racial identity or gender, share instead a commitment in growing their artistic skill sets as social change agents. Through this work with Collective Energy, I hope to extend the conversation that is already taking place around the concepts of spoken word poetry, performance, and pedagogy by remixing them together in a different way.

. . . as for me
I'm one of Chief Thundercloud, Che Guevara, Harriet Tubman's daughters
I feel right at home with my underground poetry supporters
if God be for us
that makes us unstoppable
if it looks impossible
if it sounds illogical
that keeps things exciting, we don't blink at obstacles
we don't shrink at threats
we don't rescind our statements
we don't expect you to understand if your vision ain't there yet
No matter where you come from life ain't simple
But simplicity is instrumental
heart beats the bass, keeps the tempo
there is so much I want to say to you but my words can't articulate
Clearly
If you choose to pay attention you will have to pay dearly . . .

For me, the connection of theory and praxis clicked with Carlos. Slender and soft-spoken, Carlos had a curly afro and light eyes that, combined with an ill sense of wordplay as a poet, won him favor among the ladies on campus. His peaceful demeanor and almost reverent attitude earned him my respect. He approached my desk in the cultural center with that sideways smile and greeted me with a head nod and hug.

> What's up Crystal Leigh? I just had to stop by and say thanks again for bringing that fire last night. Man, it was crazy. Thanks for letting me spit, man. Um, so I was wondering, if maybe you had some time you wouldn't mind reading over this poem I'm working on, um, you know, I could just really use a muse right now, you know? It's like, I have all these ideas and I just need to, you know what I'm saying, bounce them off of someone.

It was 11 a.m. on a Friday, and already a surprising string of visitors had stopped by my desk. I was tired from the late night before—it was the first cultural program I had ever planned in my life, and I had underestimated the toll it would take on my energy. The usual friendliness that most of my students attributed to my Southern rearing was wearing thin, and I was more than a little frustrated at the interruptions because they prevented me from accomplishing any work that required concentration. Two days of glorious poetry performances and critical cultural conversations that were a part of the Lyrical Legacies program designed by the director Toby Jenkins and the first Bed Spoken Word Lounge had satisfied an aching need that I had and also reaffirmed my confidence in my ability to perform. I had just shared the stage with the legendary Sonia Sanchez and Amiri Baraka, who were later joined by contemporary spoken word artist Ursula Rucker and hip hop all-star Black Thought, lead MC of the Roots crew, a Philly-based band that rates in the top five for conscious hip hop music. The two-day event also featured a young brother named Jason Reynolds, whom I remembered from my initial introduction to the slam poetry circuit in Baltimore, Maryland. His skill had developed astronomically, and I was moved to step up my own game as a spoken word artist after having the opportunity to reconnect with him by inviting him up to Penn State as our artist in residence.

But now it was Friday at 11 a.m. and I was drained. I had paperwork to fill out, thank-you notes to send, and deadlines to meet as a graduate assistant in the Paul Robeson Cultural Center (PRCC). Carlos was maybe the eighth student who stopped by with positive comments on the previous night. His enthusiasm and eagerness to improve his artistry stirred me, because for a brief moment I saw a flashback of myself as a twenty-one-year-old undergraduate student and poet—I thought, what if someone had just taken the time to talk to me about what to expect in the spoken word industry? What if my experience as a beginning spoken word artist and actor had been groomed by a group of friends who weren't driven only by the desire for personal gain or success but also by a deep commitment to making a change in this world?

These questions continued during a conversation over dinner with the director and my boss at the PRCC, and I jokingly shared the student feedback. Toby said she had actually invited me to dinner that day to discuss an idea she was inspired to start working on, part of which was to gather a group of student artists and create these more intense developmental experiences with me. After our meeting, modeling the collaboration we wanted from our students, Toby and I developed an outline for an integrated arts performance group that would groom artists like Carlos. Our goal was to construct a group that met on a regular basis with the hopes of growing their life skills and performance by exposing them to deeper experiences within their own campus as well as beyond. We wanted to create an environment where these student artists could correlate their personal experiences with those of their peers and use their spoken word poetry or other artistic methods to communicate those experiences to an audience. We were interested in creating a program that would allow them the chance to form and strengthen new and existing collaborative relationships in the hopes that they would practice learning from and listening to one another's perspectives. We were committed to their required participation in all the aspects of planning a program, from the set up to the tear down, and to creating regular performance opportunities for them to showcase what they were learning.

With all of these righteous intentions and meaningful learning moments built into our plans, Collective Energy was founded.

This is the "true" story . . . of eight artists . . . picked to perform
together and have their lives taped . . . to find out what happens . . .
when people stop being polite . . . and start getting real . . .
welcome to Collective Energy . . .

Spoken Word Poetry

Within these pages, I define spoken word poetry as a public poetry performance through which meaning is negotiated. Spoken word poetry is always contextualized historically and also undergoes immediate social reconstruction and reproduction during each performance. This is an important foundation to build upon because, before a performer even takes the stage, the stage itself is understood to be a contested site where negotiations of meaning and subjectivity take place. The performance of a spoken word piece implies a constant state of change. No two performances will render identical meanings, nor is that a useful goal. Although the material being performed may remain consistent, the purpose of repeated performances in different venues and contexts is to gain different perspectives and values that will drive future understandings and readings of the performance and thus the performer.

Poet laureate Billy Collins (2003) suggests that poetry performance offers a double connection: one with the poet and one with the audience. He continues, "Hearing a poem lends the experience an immediacy, a reality not found on the page" (4). The key to this triple-layered energy flow is the bodily transaction that takes place during a live performance of original work. Throughout such a performance, variable understandings and competing discourses involve some pretty serious stakes. Spoken word poetry is a performance of the struggle for power that often results in the expression of a desire for agency. No singular outcome can be guaranteed; however, there is always the likelihood that multiple and opposing interpretations of any performance will occur. Spoken word poetry invites attention to why these interpretive fractures occur, making its practice useful in identifying the various social positions inhabited by the audience and artist and the power relationships that shape the dynamic of those positions.

Performing spoken word poetry has provided Collective Energy with an outlet, a way to interrogate their views, realities, and ideas about themselves and the world around them. The act of performing their perspectives both imagined and real is an act of resistance; their performances point out instances of oppression. As the student artists write and perform in ways that directly challenge these structures, and deny the "truths" that are parroted by larger societal institutions, their art practice reworks dominant histories. By resisting the structures that work to contain and immobilize, these student artists are altering the possibilities that currently exist for working in opposition to the negative ideologies and stale solutions that they have inherited. Spoken word poetry can be utilized as a new discursive practice by marginalized youth as a means to invert the practices of power within their own social and political context.

Effective activist spoken word poetry works to open and engage, but the openings that puncture our borders cannot be measured or predicted. The more we rehearsed and worked together as a group, although our backgrounds and social positions were diverse, we realized that we experienced similar emotional reactions to experiences that touched on the humanity of us all. The more each member of Collective Energy was able to identify, explore, and even orchestrate such moments, the more critical and powerful our performance would be. Our borders were permeable; spoken word poetry performance equipped us to face and work within these vulnerabilities that are a crucial aspect of critical work.

Discourse and Performance

To appreciate and respect the transformative power of spoken word poetry is to acknowledge the role of language in maintaining power and privilege. My investigation is not to determine whether language holds power; rather, I ask whose meanings or which of the competing discourses will win. The winner is determined by the organization of social power—whoever talks the loudest and has the access to distribute their words is often who is heard. I'm suggesting that the weekly group meetings and each individual performance of Collective Energy offered us a chance to rewrite some of the dominant discourses that we named inaccurate.

In other words, by performing our personal history, the student artists are also performing the present and future, and such performance adds to the obtainable vocabulary that constructs the ways we interpret those experiences. The disparate group of characters that are outlined in the bios of Collective Energy (see the appendix) engaged first among themselves during weekly workshops to "meet, clash and grapple" with the perspectives they had been taught and the experiences they had lived (Pratt 1999, 133). Then, through intentionally taking the new knowledges formed by those friction-filled contact zones, they enveloped their audience in yet another contact zone by producing cohesive, yet not identical, politicized performances. The transaction that takes place during each of these performances calls for even more multiplicities to form as audience members create and respond during the show with interpretations of their own. Through the very act of performing as a group, Collective Energy breaks with tradition, intervening and interfering with the status quo of their environment. Challenging their status quo means resisting oppression, because each show produces narratives that offer alternatives to a master discourse that positions the student artists as powerless and disadvantaged.

Language is the vehicle of the message that is composed by the performer; however, the delivery of that message, the embodied performance, adds another layer to the already complicated performance moment. Weedon's (1997) important theoretical work establishing language as a political power provides the guts of what I am proposing as the pedagogical power that a spoken word performance has. It is the embodied performance or "acting out" that carries the message and immediately reconstructs the meaning that is embedded in the original written poem. Because of the urgent and undeniable physical situation that confronts the audience member, spoken word poetry becomes a method of mediation between the contentious dynamics at play in any given performance. Such dynamics are partly informed by the positions of the subjects—both performer and audience member—which are going to be diverse. Their positions guide the performance and lead participation, respectively, and will hopefully lead to a multiplicity of interpretations, contradictions, and understandings. An assortment of responses and recreations of performances can lead to revisions of the performance and of the subjects, providing openings and loops that indicate fluidity. Fluidity is both desirable and complicated; transforming can repel ideas of stagnation or static subjectivity, yet to have a fluid identity makes a person unwieldy to read and interact with.

Who Are You?

Another key aspect of performance is the exchange that occurs whenever artist and audience member meet. The space of the performance opens up a unique moment to explore the discourses through which their realities and meanings are negotiated. During this transaction, many things take place simultaneously, including the critical examination of ideologies and power relationships. This concept is vital to include because it implicates the audience member in the construction of each performance just as readily as the artist herself. Through spoken word poetry performance, the competing discourses that structure how and why meaning are produced not only are acknowledged but are also made visible through performance—thus creating a way to challenge identity and resist those meanings. The many subject positions that the artist and audience member take up are then available for rehearsal and further auditioning.

Subjectivities are full of energy and are never realized in a neutral or immobile state. Indeed, bell hooks (1994) reminds us how important it is for pedagogues to consider "ways to move beyond boundaries, to transgress," which implies that motion is required for any creative method of learning to take place (6). We should not assume that a "teacher" will remain an expert in her class or that a "student" is only a receptor of knowledge.

The traditional role of teacher and student was quickly disrupted at the start of our Collective Energy meetings. At one of our earliest workshop sessions, I presented a PowerPoint full of what I thought were good focus questions to articulate goals for our group. As I was the most experienced artist, I felt I had a good grasp on what we needed to focus on to develop as socially responsible artists. I was the teacher, right? I got about halfway through my presentation before I looked up and saw that every participating artist at the meeting wrinkled their noses and shook their heads. "Do you want us to take *notes*?!" asked Q. I didn't know what to do—it was the very beginning, and I was already falling back on habits from my classroom training. Tony quickly came to my rescue when he took out a piece of scratch paper and a marker and suggested that we "brainstorm our way through this." I meant well and had done my due diligence as a "facilitator" or "teacher" to come prepared with a clear plan on what the student artists needed to learn. However, that traditional role did not ask for the very investment that we were seeking from our audience members, which ironically was the topic of discussion!

Thankfully, what Collective Energy brainstormed was a very effective and inclusive list of questions adapted loosely from a reading we had all completed about activism by Yvonne Bynoe (2004). Tony's quick thinking and the group's willingness to be fluid about the course of the workshops disrupted the traditional social structures and expectations of language, teacher/student, and performer/audience. This constant shifting of roles between me and each of the student artists also yielded incredibly creative outcomes for most of our group discussions; outcomes that would never have surfaced without a commitment to critically engaging with one another as a teacher *and* a student. Although uncomfortable and new, we agreed to transgress these traditional roles and thus transform the Collective Energy workshops and rehearsal processes to spaces where we were each held accountable for our own investment. You can only get a return on what you put in.

The same is true on the scale of an artist and an audience member. We modeled the transaction during our group sessions, but the challenge was to include the same strategy during performances. According to artist/educator Charles Garoian (1999), during performance there is a transaction of language, an exchange that takes place while the subjectivity of "teacher" and "student" constantly shifts between the "artist" and "audience member" until "both are simultaneously teachers and students" (Freire in Garoian 1999, 60). When this dual role of teacher and student is acknowledged in a performance, then both audience and performer are implicated as responsible for constructing the meaning behind the language used in a performance. In other words, language is the currency of the transaction between artist and audience. What Collective Energy discovered as time passed was that not every audience member wanted the responsibility of becoming a teacher. Conflict is inevitable in performance because of the different social positions each person present inhabits, so a possible objective of spoken word is to increase awareness of these subject positions. Doing so establishes a sense of accountability for the outcome of a performance from everyone involved.

The questions that Tony jotted down as we were brainstorming that night soon became the guiding questions we turned to as we approached each new performance opportunity. We asked:

- What do we want to accomplish?
- Who has the power to control the result?
- What do they need to hear in order to act?
- Who do they need to hear it from?
- How can we ensure that voice is given to these issues?
- What do we need to develop?
- How do we know what's working?

Every time these questions were asked, the student artists put themselves in a position of reflection about the social relations that contextualize their often-oppressed reality. They authored their own questions and then used that system during our sessions to employ an assessment of checks and balances. This coconstructed list of questions was one way that the student artists tilted the imbalance of power that shaped our interactions with one another as student and teacher and also served to imbalance their relationships with the audience. A disruption of traditional roles, and the power such disruptions can yield, was particularly important as I began to examine my own position in Collective Energy. It is my hope that by articulating academically what I learned about artistically the social structures that reinforce and sustain unequal power relations will begin to be dismantled. The student artists have indeed become my teacher even as I assume a position of supposed authority.

Treasure Chest

One of the initial writing challenges posed for Collective Energy was one Toby called the Treasure Chest. The purpose of this exercise was to focus critical attention on the sources of inspiration for each student artist of Collective Energy. During our second meeting, she asked everyone to bring an item in the next week that represented a part of who they were and what motivated them to write. I explained that understanding our own motivations would assist in the shaping of our performances and we might be surprised by what we found. Stacey, who was typically pretty quiet during group discussion, was the first to volunteer to share her item for our Treasure Chest. Surprised, because I usually had to make it a point to invite her comments, I asked her to pass around the photograph she brought in. The image was of her older sister and her sister's new daughter. Again, I was surprised because Stacey was nowhere to be found in the image, with the exception of the similar features that clearly marked the girl in the photo as her sibling. We passed the photo around the room as she explained:

> STACEY: A sibling that's older, you look up to them, but it was opposite with my sister. She was always the example of what not to do. I learned a lot about myself through her, and I learned how to interact with people and interact with life.
>
> We have a different relationship. I do [love her] but I don't think I'm an emotional person, which is quite honest . . .
>
> We're on two different levels right now, but I've learned to appreciate the type of person that she is and to see we have the same qualities.
>
> CRYSTAL: What made you bring her pic for the treasure chest?
>
> STACEY: During my teenage years it was hard. We had sibling rivalry. She was the pretty one, everybody loved her, and she was the best person—I don't know . . . the cool sister, I guess you could say. Which is weird because she was the cool kid, but I had my own group, but I was more on the positive level I guess you could say? We didn't see eye to eye. We never did anything with each other. I still feel like I don't know her. We don't really talk.

Stacey's first words describing her relationship with her sister imply opposition and friction. She speaks of a sisterly relationship that is tumultuous, in which she plays a role that is contrary, yet she acknowledges that they share "the same qualities." Stacey's identification of herself as both separate and same to her sister offers an interesting site for exploring how subjectivities and discourses are constructed. What makes examining this process even more valuable is that Stacey used her position as a poet to both affirm and disrupt the ways in which she recognized herself. Helen Harper (2000) suggests, "[I]dentification involves a recognition of similarity," causing a subject to draw boundaries around the self and mark those outside such boundaries as "other." Harper elaborates, "Identification is a process of substitution and displacement . . . where we attempt to replace internally what is missing externally" (3). Stacey concedes that she and her sister are familiar because they are related by blood; however, she proceeds to list several traits such as "cool," "pretty," or "loved" by everyone that mark her as not just different from but as less than her sister. Stacey does not recognize herself as legitimately falling into any of these categories because they are unavailable to her; they are occupied by her sister. Perhaps Stacey's motivation to write and perform is derived from her ability to imagine herself inhabiting positions that she feels unable to otherwise access and to create subjectivities that may have never been vacant in her experience.

Recognition of self as a valid subject occurs during the process of being recognized by others as a valid subject. Operating as a particular subject within a particular discourse can be viewed as an activity that we partake of but do not wholly govern. In other words, Stacey refuses to participate in a discourse that would label her as "emotional"; however, she is not in a position to fully determine which discourses she gets marked as participating in. We don't always get to determine the memberships we are identified as having by others, especially when those identifying us have more power than we do. Performing her own narrative is an opportunity for Stacey to transform the subjectivities she has grown accustomed to, or been assigned. Another person may view her performance as very emotional, thus inscribing Stacey with those characteristics whether she desires them or not. Our conversation continues:

> Stacey: She made me view myself differently because I didn't do a lot of things that other people did. Back home, like, back at school people don't hang around people that don't do what you do. She brought out my best and worst. She doesn't know it and I guess I'm figuring this out myself now, but she, oh Lord, [Stacey tries not to cry], she taught me how to love myself and how to try to love other people. I'm really guarded and that's sort of how I write.

> CRYSTAL: I think that's really interesting seeing how you do write and you share it publicly. So why did you bring a picture of your sis?
>
> Q: It was the first thing she saw on the dresser.
>
> STACEY: [crying now] I think I brought this because with Victoria (her niece) because of the baby—now I don't see her as my sister. I see her as a mother; because we're close in age that's difficult for me to see. It represents someone I wish I knew but will probably never get to know.

Stacey continues to express a desire for intimacy with her sister in a relationship that is socially structured to fulfill such a need. She is determined to connect herself to her performance of spoken word in order to make whole what she views as a lack. Although she is the younger sibling, Stacey mentioned earlier her older sister's example of "what not to do," making Stacey feel the need to remove or demarcate herself from that example. While the audience may not substantiate Stacey's subjectivity, her performance and imagining authenticates it for her. Stacey comments that she sees herself as "guarded" and that she feels disconnected from her poetry in the same way. Stacey's choice to bring in this image of her sister and her sister's child signifies another desire: to be more emotionally expressive. It was difficult for me to hear this passionate artist describe a void that she associated with her defense mechanisms while being vulnerable enough to shed tears in front of the group during one of our first meetings. The photograph stands for difference in Stacey's life, and that difference is painful because it implies *distance*. The absence and loss that identify Stacey's subjectivity are also driving motivators for the ways in which she aims to use her spoken word performance.

Performance functions in this way as an attempt to make connections between the discourses she willingly takes part in and those that distinguish her as uncool, unpretty, and separate. Stacey uses spoken word poetry as a way to "assert difference . . . in all its forms and manifestations, to find a commonality in the experience of difference without compromising its distinctive realities and effects" (Gentile in Orner 1992, 85). In other words, Stacey is acknowledging her different and sometimes negative subjectivities through her performance and through the ways she contributed to Collective Energy. Stacey then acts out her difference, possibly as a mode of seeking alliance and connection with others who also inhabit or are assigned "different" subjectivities. Spoken word poetry then becomes a tool for Stacey to distinguish herself, affirm her experiences of the consequences of her difference, and to make useful connections across the categories in which she is cast, providing her with agency and making tangible the social boundaries she abides within. Performance also illuminates the spaces where those boundaries are porous, making her subjectivities blurry and indistinct at times, blending and separating Stacey's reality and imagination at different junctures. There is the chance for a great deal of personal mobility within such a performance practice. Stacey's story is one example of the multiple roles the members of Collective Energy were cast in—and the casting was not simply passive, for Stacey cast herself there, too. Our identities were scribed by the audience and by our performances. Stacey demonstrates the process of recognizing herself as a subject through performance. She was busy learning to understudy for a variety of particular positions, as was I. Exercising new subjectivities is significant because it provided Stacey and me a place to experiment with a variety of roles should we desire to alter or adjust our positions.

Because spoken word poetry performance is an embodied mode of inquiry, in order to be effective, it is important to address the ways in which my body performs for an audience before I open my mouth to share a poem. My body may be interpreted as telling a story that my words contradict. This point leads me to the concept of "passing" that I find myself continually returning to, mostly because I have passed on many occasions for numerous people. Passing is how I navigate the world I live in, because it occasionally allows me to either squeeze past conflict or to manipulate conflict. This privileged contradiction and performance has been the source for the majority of the splits in myself that I have experienced and that I have intentionally kept separate. Evelyn Alsultany (2002) speaks effectively to the logic that shapes such splinters:

> My identity fractures as I experience differing dislocations in multiple contexts. Sometimes people otherize me, sometimes they identify with me. Both situations can be equally problematic. Those who otherize me fail to see a shared humanity and those who identify with me fail to see difference. (107)

The "either/or" option is unacceptable because it is both false and limiting as a dichotomy and it excludes the multifaceted variety that composes my subjectivity. Another issue is that I have been forced to respond to others according to the response that my body and my being provoke from them.

I am never the one that raises the issue of identity politics within a conversation; typically, I skirt around it. Because of this, my response has not been an active one; my response has been "passive," similar to the way that I have "passed" through life, through expectations, through society. I have grown tired of this feeling. It is exhausting to be required to justify my very existence and to locate myself so that others know how to interact with me. As a result of this common experience, what has become clear is that fluidity is something desirable, a skill to be developed rather than denied. A willingness to adapt or to adjust behavior in accordance with one's environment is an ability that is demanded of most people of color, commonly understood as a "double consciousness" as defined by Frantz Fanon (1967) in his expansion of W. E. B. Du Bois's work on race and society. Du Bois (1903) explains that having a double consciousness for an African American male is "this sense of always looking at one's self through the eyes of others, of measuring one's soul by the tape of a world that looks on in amused contempt and pity" (4). While Du Bois was speaking specifically to the division that he perceived between being Black, male, and American, Fanon focuses that idea by suggesting that "the black man has two dimensions: one with his fellows, the other with the white man" (17). Fanon goes on to remark that mastering language affords remarkable power (1967, 18). Imagine then how much more extensive and complicated this process of fracturing identity and self can be for those of us who embody and exist on multiple ethnic and sexual planes at once. The fractures that Alsultany (2002) designates are a result of succumbing to and perpetuating the illusion that Brookes (1992) titled a deadly lie. Coping to survive may keep us in motion, and it seems that performance supplies us with tools to explore the cracks of our composure.

Similar to Stacey's earlier example, Tony also used spoken word as a way to move between the multitudes of subject positions that he acknowledges. His lesson on fluidity and fracturing also stems from the item he brought to share for the Treasure Chest activity. The story behind Tony's item, like Stacey's, centers on a lesson he has learned from an influential family member.

> TONY: In 1995, my Uncle Tony passed away from AIDS—when I was visiting him two days before he died, I was telling him,

> "I need a wallet." He was like, "What you need a wallet for? You young, you ain't got no money." [laughter from the whole group] And I was like, I do have money. He said, "Alright, well, when you go back to your grandma's house, look in this drawer next to my bed and there's a wallet in there. You can have that one." I said, "Cool." So I went to grandma's house that same night, opened up his drawer, and inside was this really cool wallet, but there was a crisp, really clean one dollar bill inside. I looked at the dollar and thought why is this random one dollar bill in here? So the next day I went back to the hospital, and I said, "Uncle Tony," except I used to call him UT for short. So I said, "UT, I found this one dollar bill in your wallet." He said, "Good, you should keep that cuz although on the surface it says 'one' the dollar bill is four quarters, and it's also twenty nickels, and it's also ten dimes, and it's also one hundred pennies." He said, no matter what, people always look at you like you're just a dollar, but there is so much more. Like, so many more pieces to you. Like, never just defining yourself by what's on your face. So I've been—so I framed—laminated that one dollar bill; I've never touched it or spent it.
>
> Obviously what I'm learning about myself is that there is so much more to me. And sometimes people just see this [waves dollar]. Um, so that's what I wanted to bring and show . . .

This snapshot of Tony's life is almost overwhelming in the host of thoughts, questions, and feelings that it reveals. As one of Tony's closest friends, I have never heard him mention this story, or his uncle, outside of this one incident. During his membership in Collective Energy, none of Tony's poems explicitly dealt with HIV/AIDS. The lesson being taught here is clear: you are more than your surface, or in poststructural terms, you are more than the subjectivities you are assigned or choose to take up. His uncle was also teaching him about interpellation and recognition—some folks "look at you like you're just a dollar"—and Tony has since worked to refuse "just defining yourself by what's on your face." As a young African American male, this wisdom passed on by his older uncle is instruction that is particularly salient. Spoken word poetry has functioned for Tony as a way to measure and recognize himself as a subscriber to various discourses; it creates a space and opportunity for him to demonstrate "that there is so much more" to him, even when others only glimpse his surface. On a larger scale, performing as a unit full of divergent subjectivities and a crisscross of experiences in each show was good practice in switching places for Collective Energy.

Another theme present here is the various combinations of coins that can work together to equal an entire dollar. It's possible that Tony's uncle was using this example to refer not only to the many parts of Tony as an individual but also to remind him that his family members had each contributed in some way to Tony's overall worth. If a dollar is missing even a penny, then it ceases to be a dollar.

Tony represents for his family a first-generation college student, a performer, and he has successfully completed a graduate degree at a major university. In a not-so-subtle way, Tony's dollar was a reminder to him that the appearance of wholeness that a single dollar gives is an illusion. By climbing the ranks of higher education and working steadily to earn respect through his academic work, Tony has sought the mobility and power that can be afforded by "mastering the language," as Fanon said (1967, 18). Tony has performed as a college student and an employee, operating in traditional discourses of success, and has at the same time disrupted the social ideals that fuel the definition of those same discourses by writing his own. He is aware that he is not one cohesive, whole entity but can be made whole through many different combinations that have been assigned differing values by the weighted scale of the society in which he lives. He uses spoken word to resist the value assignments placed upon his experience, his family, and himself.

Spoken word poetry performance has served him in this way as a method to subversively rebel against those assignments, at the same time affirming his experience and perspective. Spoken word has provided Tony with a way to challenge those who would judge him just by "what's on his face," while he also has actively participated in the practices (such as attending graduate school) that previously excluded African American men. By constructing his own performances to create new combinations of roles to participate in, Tony has effectively recognized himself and worked to rearrange what he wants to change. Tony sometimes uses his performance as a way to confront and challenge how others see him and the way that the matrix of domination has organized his life (Collins 1991). Highly intelligent wordplay, references to overlooked historical facts, and dynamic delivery are skills that Tony calls upon during his performance. Illusion disintegrates with each line that he pronounces on stage. He energizes stagnant possibilities for hope and charges those who witness his performance to take action.

Black Man's Call to Action

Tony Keith

Words have power

Letters are electrically charged and when bounded together create enough energy to cause massive explosions

Blowing massive mountain tops into tiny metaphorical erosions

And it is I that stands atop one of those mounds

With words, phrases, vowels, syllables, and sounds, and I'm screaming:

THIS IS FOR ALL OF YA'LL STILL DREAMING!

Those of you whose hue starts off as Black until you've been beaten down to blue

Don't know who the f*ck you are cuz you're busy letting society define you

Ain't got a pot to piss in, a window to throw it out of, or no food to chew

And so you're starving

Starving for knowledge

Not cuz you can't grasp the language but cuz no one took the time to teach you

They claim you're too stubborn to listen to

Your head's too thick to even get a brick through

That you're nothing but a no good, pants sagging, baby making, juvenile delinquent

All that you're capable to do is eat, sleep, shyt, and screw

BUT BROTHERS I HAVE SOMETHING DIFFERENT TO TELL YOU!

And I invoke in my self the spirit of everything African within me

From my forehead to my collarbone

From my bloodstream to my skin tone

From my strong back to my humble knees

From my shinbone to my callused feet

AND I DECLARE YOU FREE!

No longer property

No longer a weapon for society to continue to arm you with massive missiles of misguided perceptions of manhood into your looking glasses

So F*CK sitting in the back writing R.I.P. to your friends on that dirty desk you're now in the front teaching classes

So F*CK being afraid to use slang; I'm granting you the right to use the language of your people to move the masses

And F*CK waiting in the back of the line to get to the front; I'm giving you a lifetime supply of free V.I.P. back-stage passes

And if I someone says you didn't pay your way, say F*CK you, it's already being deducted from my taxes

And if they need some proof, tell them they can find it printed on the receipts of paper made from trees once used to whip the back of slave's asses

And if they still have questions, tell them you can call up the Black Men's Headquarters and have them send that shyt out through smoke signals or Morse code dashes

And if they still have questions, tell them to take a pin, and prick your skin and check your deoxyribonucleic acid—better known as your D.N.A.

BECAUSE THEY DON'T NEED ANSWERS

THEY DON'T NEED ANYTHING

And if they do—tell them to come see me cuz Brothers I got you

I'm holding ya'll up on my shoulders to give you a higher view

And I'm carrying ya'll through mountain tops and through muddy waters, and don't worry, cuz historically, I've been known to split that shyt in two . . .

This piece symbolized a sort of breakthrough for Tony. This was one of the very first poems he wrote and delivered in an aggressive, unapologetic style. Tony's performance prior to this poem was very diplomatic. He took a risk in this piece by boldly pointing out the illusions confirming their existence and then offering an alternative. Spoken word poetry functions for Tony here as a method of recognizing himself as an autonomous, authoritative young Black man. He names himself author of freedom for the young Black men listening to him. He begins by listing the traits often ascribed to young Black men, such as "lazy" and "stubborn" "juvenile delinquents" whose sole ability lies in their practice of consumption, production of waste, and careless baby-making. Then, he boldly denies each and every one of these categories on his own authority. He calls upon his cultural heritage and stands upon nothing except his birthright as an African American to rebuke the negative stereotypes projected onto young men of color. He invites them to participate in other subjectivities that share in the authority he has taken as a way to resist "the misguided perceptions of manhood" that are made available.

Tony used "Black Man's Call to Action" as a way to confront his frustrations with the view of the "surface" that he once identified with and, as Althusser (1971) reminds us, answered to. Tony's poem calls up sameness by addressing a broad yet varied category of people unified only by a racial thread that signifies home and a sense of familiarity of experience. At the same time, he also works to establish difference by othering his participation as a member in the subjecthood of "Black men." Tony subverts the ways he is expected by society to enact his role as a "Black man." In other words, he makes use of the "surface," of "what's on his face," to gather his audience under one banner and then disrupt that unity by isolating the smaller units that create the whole. In this way, Tony uses spoken word poetry to rebel against the same discourses he willingly takes part in—so they will be overlapped with new and different discourses that provide better options for his objectives. Tony works to counter the very culture he participates in by singing his own melody throughout the illusion of harmony.

Social transformation, then, begins to take place when the performers or student artists are able to renegotiate a way of making meaning that no longer situates them in a victimized state. Rather, their repositioning or realignment of their position, even if imagined, changes the social and material narratives that have scribed them at least within a certain time and space. By exercising agency in this way, they develop the ability to teach others (such as audience members) the same technique. Through the creation and recreation of subjectivity, the student artists produce new readings of old, oppressive texts and tell new stories within stale social constraints. Spoken word performance provides a way to be seen and heard for students whose concerns, lives, and dreams are often unheeded. Realizing an active relationship between artist and audience is key for enlarging the scope that performance provides to view the effects of social injustices. The oppressive sense of isolation that often results from experiences of injustice or inequality can potentially be identified and altered once these personal experiences are located within the structural divisions that determine material aspects of social existence. Performing spoken word makes available a discourse through which an alternate picture of such structures can be seen. Like a smudged, cracked mirror, the visions that can be seen are not always seen clearly, nor is seeing or hearing quite enough. However, once these structures are identified and their consequences are taken seriously and understood in relation to personal experiences, then new plans of action (or strategies) can be devised in order to promote social change.

If we hone in for a moment on the issues of autobiographical interrogations that spoken word poetry can induce, then Collective Energy performances can be situated as a means of self-inquiry and knowledge production because of the audiences' interpretation of a performance that is at once fiercely personal and unabashedly public. Each historical moment in which a spoken word piece is performed will render a new version or translation of the artists' autobiographies. What makes Collective Energy so powerful is that it provides the space and focused time to examine those subject positions and impose new and plural meanings upon them. Our experiences together still operate for me like a palimpsest, an old scroll or writing tablet that is used again and again after old writing has been erased. Collective Energy is the tablet as much as the writings for me, and the stages we shared continue to impact the work that I do with students around the world teaching them how to utilize the arts as tools for empowerment. So I ask, what does this mean for pieces that are developed collaboratively? For no matter how metaphorical or abstract the language used, no matter how delicate the melody and unified the harmony, the majority of content refers to an experience or idea that is seeded in the life of the student artists.

This is my effort to reconcile the separation of mind, body, and spirit that is so often demanded by academic work (Brookes 1992; Dehli 1991; Rockhill

1987). This is also an effort to refocus the lens through which audiences will read this work. It is a means to pay tribute to the emotion, desire, pain, and pleasure that constitute the conditions of my being here (Dehli 1991, 64). This is another way that I acknowledge that I am my home—I am a bridge, a conduit, and most certainly a medium.

In her poetic and profound work on third world women and the *mestiza* consciousness, Gloria Anzaldúa (1981) writes of a quest for the "center of the self" that has been alienated due to an internalized exile that women of color experience (p. 169). She argues that writing helps us to survive that exile and alters our alien status. It is such a return to the center of many selves that I find myself fumbling towards in the dusk of the day, a careful searching for tender gaps that were rent in the split of myself when I first realized I was "Other," in those moments before I realized I could choose to be "Other" or not. In performance, I find a space similar to the battle ground and sanctuary that Anzaldúa finds in writing.

This is what I have tried to share with Collective Energy. The discovery that I was not alone in my performance experiences emboldened me as an artist, and I was excited at the idea of throwing in my lot with other artists. I had never been a part of such a group—I had not even written a collaborative poem before—yet I found the idea of artistic companionship appealing because of how isolating I found my experience as a student and an artist myself.

I'm getting to tell a story that until now, I did not believe I was capable of telling. Collective Energy does validate me, but only because I was a part of it. I didn't earn the right to tell this story because I'm a woman of color, or working class, or first generation college student, or an artist. I earned the calling because I was given permission to tell the story by those involved—including myself. I name myself author.

Gloria Anzaldúa (1981) explains what naming oneself author means in words that I feel ringing in my own hands:

> Why am I compelled to write? Because the writing saves me from this complacency I fear. Because the world I create in the writing compensates for what the real world does not give me. By writing I put order in the world, give it a handle so I can grasp it. I write because life does not appease my appetites and hunger. I write to record what others erase when I speak, to rewrite the stories others have miswritten about me, about you. To become more intimate with myself and you. To convince myself that I am worthy and that what I have to say is not a

> pile of shit. Finally, I write because I'm scared of writing but I'm more scared of not writing. (169)

For me, this attempt to share the work of the student artists who perform with Collective Energy is a demonstration of the bridges that Anzaldúa and her comrades demanded be acknowledged. Anzaldúa writes to know herself and to know the reader, just as the spoken word artist performs to learn herself, her audience, and her world. It is an effort to move somewhere beyond salvaging the remains offered by an oppressive and bitter system and toward our wildest imaginations, because sometimes, what we can dream, oversights included, is all that pushes us on. Collective Energy was built on such dreams.

"Doing" Research

As we began the journey of what was to become Collective Energy and a PRCC tradition, I was anxious about the leadership and researcher positions I was to play. I was leery of the responsibility that both of these positions were burdened with. The disappearing act or false sense of objectivity is simply not possible due to my position and the role that I played in forming, planning, and finally controlling the aspects of the research that I chose to present. The logistical planning that is required by any student affairs program added to my already heavy load the duties of budgeting, supervising, negotiating, and reporting results to my superiors. These duties clearly distinguished me from the group as a leader and sometimes a mentor, and, because of this role, because of my personal stake in the recording of our time together, it was impossible for the other members of Collective Energy to ignore our distinctions.

What I did eventually come to find as central was transparency about the power—which is a practice that has continued to help me as I grow in a faculty role as well. I learned that honesty was key, and as such, I had to clearly communicate to the research subjects that it was my desire to share not only in the power of planning but also in the responsibility of what would be produced in the research space. The same is true for the artist and the audience member—accountability rests with both. The insider/outsider nature of my roles requires me to be in constant communication about my objectives with the student artists and with my audience.

While the student artists were aware that the video recordings of our sessions and performances and the copies of their notebooks would compile my research, it didn't seem to impact their desire to share. The presence of the camera only amplified the playful banter that was always happening during our time together. They certainly didn't shy away from the camera. Because of their nonchalant reactions to my constant reminders that I was going to use their words and work to get my diploma, I think it is important to view the space and time we shared as a research space as well as a space for cultural production. Although at times these spaces overlap or edge one another out, the effects they had on me were distinctive.

I found myself developing the characters of artist and researcher/leader and sometimes failing at changing up my costume at the appropriate time. I felt responsible for achieving my ideas of success for our group, which initially included each member claiming to be an activist/artist by the end of the project. I didn't realize that just like teaching in a college classroom, facilitating a group like Collective Energy might not yield tangible results for me. For example, I was disappointed when the group didn't respond to a particular prompt or performance opportunity in the way I predicted they might. It wasn't until most of us had graduated from Penn State that I first received positive feedback that they were still benefiting from their time spent in Collective Energy. It wasn't until after Stacey graduated that she texted me at 11 p.m. after winning her first poetry slam in her hometown of Philadelphia. I was so proud, and so honored that she thought to share her victory with me. As an artist, I never had to seriously consider if my performance had any lasting impact or aftereffects. With Collective Energy, just like with the traditional classes I taught, it mattered to me so much. Jonathan, Tony, and Q all pursued a career in the field of education (high school through college level). Alyssa continues to work in the nonprofit sector as well. We stay in touch. I fumbled with the shift in my roles with these student artists precisely because I cared but had no training for how to manage my emotional investments. There was no way to measure the reach of an arts experience like the one we shared.

Yet, even though I conducted Collective Energy, I did not have complete autonomy over the group. I didn't always get to choose when I performed which role for them. There were plenty of moments my judgments or desires were overruled despite my position as leader because I was also only a graduate assistant. Aside from being flexible around the student artists and their ideas and contributions, I was also leading the program because it was my job and I was responsible for the results. While Toby created a work environment that was incomparable to any I have experienced before or since, and she trained me to be excellent as a cultural programmer, she was still my boss. I answered to her in the chain of command, and while she graciously always referred to us as a team, Toby was unquestionably in authority as the director of the PRCC. So even though I was "in charge" of leading the meetings, I did not have full control, and thus the process taught me to be flexible enough to adjust to the student artists' feedback in addition to Toby's input. At the same time, I spent hours each day in classrooms as a student, which served as a constant reminder that my experiences as a woman of color in a graduate program on a predominantly White campus marginalized me. Inside these classes I was either the token and expected to speak for every person of color, or I was silenced and actively excluded. Learning how to read a situation, how to code-switch quickly, to be limber in my performances, and flexible in my expectations grew increasingly important for my personal survival. I was overwhelmed and unsteady. This is another reason why creating opportunities to perform spoken word became increasingly important to me—as an artist I found liberation (however brief) from these hierarchies. Sometimes the stage minimalized and disregarded me further, and other times, I was the king of the world. Spoken word poetry is what helped me struggle with balancing my identities, synthesizing my saturation and drought of power in lucid moments on stage.

At first, I tried to think up ways to reduce the impact all of these subject positions might have in regard to my attempts to construct a democracy and to invite participation and feedback from everyone involved. What I came to realize instead was that my subject positions and the perspectives they gave me were important to include. While this may sound basic and foundational, it was quite a profound moment of epiphany for me; how could I create a space that liberated and facilitated communication and honesty if I was downplaying the multiple roles that I was striving to fill? By acknowledging the stresses of this position and the added sense of obligation and efforts I was making, I was demonstrating how to use the space we created together as place where vulnerability was not only possible but safe and desired.

I was new to "doing" research, but I had a great deal of experience when it came to "doing" social justice performance work. Indeed, my own existence as an artist and my own production of knowledge within our group meetings and my cultural production through our performances instantly throw Collective Energy into the category of a participatory project, for it was from the overflowing fountain of "everyday life experience and feelings" that we drew bucket after bucket of inspiration for songs, poems, and themes for discussion.

During our group meetings, it became evident that consciousness-raising was an important part of the immediate experience of Collective Energy. The reason for presenting bits of this research to a broad audience through spoken word and theater performances and articles that will be read by my own academic peers, as well as to a greater audience, is to raise awareness of both the similarities and the differences in our experiences. I hope to incite some consideration, some thought of communication, some effort toward inclusion, some outreach, some increased sensitivity to those of us who struggle to embody and execute a life dedicated to action. The project here is to present a thoroughly investigated portion of what such a life might look like for the purpose of bettering practices of educational, artistic, and activist nature.

. . . wanna teach the youngsters
better manners good grammar
family planning
avoid negativity like internet spamming
living life reckless
lash out at those who can help you because you feel helpless
it won't solve the problem
only buries the seed of dissatisfaction deep
so that even if you control it in the daytime nightmares get you when
you sleep
i know it's hard to speak
with respect in a world that shows you little
but give a little
humble head bow as you ask for what you need
pride is brittle
and most often pride won't land you on your feet
developing maturity
comes at a high cost
most are eager for the glory
but are ignorant of the loss,
to be truly great, sacrifices are made
everyday
still, folks throw it away, say thanks for keeping me entertained
they can't see past the energy to the pain
so if you do what you to validate
it's going to be a tough lesson, baby
a hard road, honey
the talent might carry you to a place your moral fiber can't keep you
then down comes the church, down comes the steeple
and who suffers most of all
whenever a great person falls?
The PEOPLE . . .

This is the difficult part. Sharing the times that I was frustrated with my own lack of progress or inability to connect even the simplest of lessons to life is not necessarily hard to do, but it is painful. I strategized my lesson plans and steered the group discussions because I was convinced that there was a place we all needed to go together. Sometimes our group sessions took a turn toward the confessional. Self-revelation onstage was one thing, but in our workshops it complicated and fogged up a lens that started out very sharply outlining my aims in this project both as a researcher and a member of Collective Energy. Looking back, I see that I cannot call my own spoken word poetry activist and then neglect to utilize my academic studies in the same way. Looking back, I realize that I am also looking ahead to the future possibilities that my personal/political/professional goals might be fulfilled because of who and what I see reflected and prioritized behind me.

As I stated before, one of my main personal obligations is to the broad audience that may never have an opportunity to enter the walls of a university or college, and perhaps through participating in some version or format of this text they can imagine doing so. By locating myself and the other student artists in a position to speak in an academic text, it is my hope that the sounds we make might resonate with the current conversations and interchanges around socially responsible artistry.

The unfortunate reality is that art is viewed as an embellishment, as decoration, a frivolous (albeit beautiful) addition to academic work and to life in general. Art and culture are "fun" but unnecessary, a luxury that one can live without. I want the representation of my research to be reflective of the lived experiences it is drawn from. The life of the action researcher, then, is similar to that of the teaching artist. If an artist who is also a teacher must make provisions in order to have time, energy, resources, inspiration, rest, and opportunities to create art, then the teaching artist will commit to disciplining herself around those needs. When an ideology is adopted or when a human being has certain values, she will strive to align her behavior with those values. Indeed, one of the renderings of a/r/tography is contiguity, which places special importance upon the "ideas that lie adjacent to one another, touch one another, or exist in the presence of one another . . . the artist, researcher and teacher identities existing simultaneously and alongside one another" (Irwin and Springgay 2008, xxvii). Instead of trying to delineate a marked and static determination between these existences, living practice and inquiry requires instead that these "in-between spaces" are cultivated and viewed as valuable connections. Collective Energy originates from the in-between space. What a relief.

Caring for one another, caring for ourselves, and how that translates into the jobs we take and the ways we spend our free time (which is not so free after all) are all factors in our happiness, in our resistance, and in our peace of mind.

As a young female artist of color, moments of intense isolation and loneliness are frequent for me. Spoken word poetry was for me always a way to assert my existence, a way to shed the urge to "belong" and to take up the mantle of rightful existence and entitlement to be where I am, in both university and society. Pioneering feminist scholars and community activists have worked hard to remind us that marginalized students struggle to keep from disappearing (see Hansberry 1971; hooks 2001; Irigaray 1985). I endeavor to be seen by others so that I know I exist; spoken word poetry functions for me in this way because it refuses me a demure or apologetic entrance into the visible and verbal. I assume and understand that some of the members of Collective Energy experience a transformation similar to mine while onstage, and I wanted to utilize the weekly meetings to supplement the few performance opportunities we had at Penn State. Even though the self-portraits we sketched were only drawn in pencil, I wanted to eliminate any erasers of outside privilege that worked to smear them, or at least provide the student artists with some different angles with which to see their own reflections. Similarly to Helen J. Harper (2000), I ask: How can we possibly intervene effectively on a college campus, in a classroom, or a community using the power of spoken word poetry performance and identification in a project of social transformation? What are the openings a project like this provides for student artists? In what ways does it complicate their lives? What sorts of artistic and pedagogical practices might best serve the students and practitioners that seek to participate in developing programs like Collective Energy? These questions and the lessons we learned throughout the year shape this inquiry and continue to guide the workshops I create and the research that I do. Up to this point, I had certainly never led any sort of class like this before. Impatient as I was to begin, I felt the small hard ball of doubt rolling around the pit of my stomach that was to stay there throughout the entire experience—after all, who did I think I was?

2

From the Inside Out

The Set

Rebel artist and legendary community activist Guillermo Gómez-Peña and Roberto Sifuentes (2011) suggest that performance surely "carries a transformative seed, a seed that nests in the psyche of the audience and slowly grows in the weeks and months following the event," and this is the thrust of the argument for spoken word poetry performance as an effective tool for social change. However, Gómez-Peña and Sifuentes continue to argue that it is the actual teaching, learning, and practice of developing the new performance materials—which was the focus of each Collective Energy workshop—that is the "most transformative and hopeful aspect" of performance work (6). This perspective prioritizes the process as more important than the product. The audience may thrill at the electrified three-and-a-half-minute performance of a spoken word artist, but the process leading up to those few moments on stage is what offers us deeper insight into how to best develop practices of socially responsible art and performance. The process of development deserves attention and offers effective lessons about what it means to build community and develop relationships with other artists. By examining the process, I was able to identify the important components necessary for designing a community, assessing the effectiveness of that creative process, and understanding how the student artists perceived their own roles in collaborative creative work that is socially responsible. I was also able to identify parallels between the Collective Energy workshops and the structure of my more traditional classroom practices, where I attempted a conscious effort to ensure critical pedagogy was taking place.

Social Responsibility

When I first invited these student artists to participate in this project, I developed an outline that centered on Maulana Karenga's (2003) theory known as "social artistic responsibility." This outline was the focus of our very first workshop together. His theory states,

> Socially responsible artistic expression must meet three qualifications: (1) it must be functional, possessing the ability to address social issues particularly affecting oppressed and marginalized communities (2) it must be collective, representing the fullness of the cultural experience of a people and (3) it must be committing, offering forth a motivation for the realization of a people's true potential and an active work against social limitations. (Karenga 1997)

While Karenga's ideas drove the foundation for Collective Energy, throughout the year there was also ongoing discussion and debate within Collective Energy about what could be counted as social responsibility. During our first workshop, the following discussion ensued after I asked the group what their thoughts were on Karenga's theory.

> CARLOS: I don't think this is the end-all be-all.
>
> Q: The first thing that came to my head was that it must be something political, um, but I guess once you look past what the words are actually saying, he's basically saying to reveal hidden ideologies or just bring forth the truth. And seemingly to me, that's what poetry or artistic expression is about.
>
> CARLOS: Maybe we should be working toward representing the fullness of a cultural experience. I'm picturing like whoever the artist is, not doing it half-ass. You're going to attempt to represent the fullness, not that you always are going to be able to do that or represent everything. But trying to—
>
> Q: I think it means from a personal perspective—represent exactly what you experience—

Q's thoughts on Karenga's guidelines point to a very interesting intersection that the student artists continued to trouble. She begins by saying social responsibility "must be something political" and elaborates that she interprets it to be an act of revelation, "bring[ing] forth the truth." After a bit more thought, she continues to flesh out her idea, suggesting that Karenga is speaking of social responsibility "from a personal perspective," and that this requires artists to "represent exactly what you experience." Her observations are interesting to note for several reasons.

Q's first statement, "it must be something political," hints at the suggestion that there is a possibility of *not* being political as an artist. In her work on the political effectiveness of popular culture, Marisa Kula (2002) also cautions artists against "assum[ing] work is interpreted in political ways if authors resist placing the work in a definite political context" (59). Q then turns to her personal experience and says that performing about her own experience is a demonstration of social responsibility. What concerned me was the disconnect that seemed to occur when Q defined what counted as "political"; she would not assign her personal experience that title. While her ideas suggest feminist foundations that assume the personal is political, I was troubled by the way she delineated the two realms. I was deeply anxious to ensure Q's level of comfort during Collective Energy because she was brand new to writing and performing, and she was also a new women's studies major during that first semester of Collective Energy. I found myself attempting to protect her from the reactions of an unpredictable audience and her stage fright, encouraging her to return to her notebook again and again. I was the instructor for her first women's studies class, and I consciously invited her to verbally contribute to the classroom conversations as well. Q's other major was criminal justice, which added another texture to her writing and conversation. I wasn't sure Q counted her personal experience as worthwhile, because she was hesitant to share in both public spaces. The stage and the classroom both seemed to intimidate her. To me it sounded as if she didn't think her experience counted as political when, in fact, everything is political. What I realize now is that if Q didn't understand her locations within a variety of contexts that implicated each of her performances as political, then I felt responsible. Her cultural production as an immigrant Caribbean woman in a Western academic context offers a critical analysis about the outcome of her experience, including the social institutions that structure her experience. Her physical and social location within a largely hegemonic campus environment that values status quo makes her presence as a woman and as a "foreigner" disruptive without any additional verbal contribution. Q's decision to speak up in class discussions and to perform onstage increase the danger she is in for resisting and posing a threat to the dominant narrative of the institution in which she is located. In every performance that she chooses to speak about her personal history, Q invites a powerful cultural critique as she performs.

Returning to Karenga's ideas, Q's insight brought to light another issue. It is extremely difficult and a bit insulting to assume that a single artist is able, no matter how great the artist, to identify with and "represent the fullness of the cultural experience of a people." Our aim was to produce art and performances that show a multiplicity of perspectives and experiences. Because of this goal, we were unable to subscribe to the belief that it could possibly be our responsibility to generalize the experience of any one of our cultures. We could never hope, nor did we desire to presume, to speak for all of those who may identify themselves as members of our culture. Q suggested that the socially responsible artist might find it possible to "represent exactly what you experience," which is a tall bill to fit. I turn to Mimi Orner (1992) to address the false hope of total representation:

> If our subject positions, versions of history, and interpretations of experiences are seen as temporary and contingent understandings within an ongoing process in which any absolute meaning or truth is impossible, then our voicing of our differences ought not be received as if we are speaking some solemn Truth about our lives. (86)

The ever-changing reality through which we negotiate our identities necessitates the meanings we reach as "temporary" and partial. Articulating our differences then does not confine us; instead, these performances zoom in on particular intersections of time and space that dissipate like smoke. It is clear from her statements that Q values honesty; however, being honest and being expected to tell the complete Truth about anything is impossible. By describing the value of these acts of "revelation," as she puts it, Q is emphasizing that a socially responsible artist will address what they have gone through in "real life" accounts of their experience. Learning about "the ideological frame of reference through which people attempt to deal with the circumstances in which they find themselves" is important to Q, because it offers her a chance to explore someone else's tactics for survival and apply them to her own life (Mullings in Collins 1991, 163). Q was excited to practice the act of revelation through exposing her own personal experiences. Performing spoken word poetry was a way for her to rehearse and reconsider her choices and circumstances before deciding to discuss them in a traditional classroom setting. Rehearsing her oppression and acts of resistance on stage gave Q a chance to reflect and unpack her personal choices in a creative way before examining them through academic theory that she complained left her cold or simply did not apply. More importantly, by using her life experiences as an immigrant, as a woman of color, and her strategies for survival as content of her performance pieces, Q used the stage to legitimize her story—a story that up to this point, she had not heard echoes of through any academic texts we had read in class.

Q also listed "exposing hidden ideologies" as part of the requirements of a socially responsible artist. Q's hunger for a "real" story of "real" experience speaks to the shortage of examples and role models for what a socially responsible feminist or activist artist looks like and the sorts of stories a socially responsible artist may tell. The appeal of spoken word poetry for Q is the opportunity it provides for her to share her own examples from her "personal perspective." In this way, performance validates those experiences she wishes to share that may not be readily available through mainstream popular cultures. Such validation is particularly important because such examples are not readily available for a young woman occupying Q's subject positions. Q wanted to relate; she wanted to connect.

What I came to realize was that Q was not looking for the static Truth as I initially thought—instead, she wanted to examine the perspectives of others that were performed honestly and use what others produced to inspire her own version of history. Q's version of history as she chooses to perform it is explicitly political, because it is within performance that her agency lies; there she poses a threat to the "hidden ideologies" that she associates with Karenga's definition. Spoken word was a way for her to take control of her narrative and of the representations accessible to her and her peers. As Q gained more experience on stage, she also grew more comfortable in the classroom setting. Instead of me calling on her, Q started volunteering in class. Q was deliberately moving into a more powerful and authoritative position through her own volition. Q wanted to teach.

Q's position as a socially responsible agent and artist marks her as dangerous, because through performance she has the potential to expose the disguised ideologies that work to confine and restrict her movement. Her power is in her resistance and willingness to take that chance, her enthusiasm to utilize her position as "the threat [and] the knowledge of the possibility that black women can embody and relate a credible version of history" (Martin 1996, 91). Q's engagement with performance was exploratory at this point in our conversations because she was a beginner at writing and sharing her poetry. Her eagerness to grow her skills at composing pieces with precise language is heartening. Q remains one of the most committed student artists of Collective Energy. She is not shy about her goals to improve and explore how spoken word poetry functions in her life.

Commitment

Carlos also voiced specific views in this particular exchange about Karenga's theories, particularly in regard to issues of commitment. He suggested that the socially responsible artist would be consistently "working towards" representing the experiences of a community, which implies that there is not necessarily a finishing place or stopping point. Carlos elaborates on his expectations of social responsibility as an artist who will "attempt" to achieve the goal of "fullness" while understanding that she or he may never be capable of doing so. In the broader context of Collective Energy's experience, what might this effort that is not "half-ass" look like? Carlos's stance was firm regarding the socially responsible artists' "trying to," which also indicates his expectation that the socially responsible artist be a highly disciplined and self-motivated artist. Carlos paints a dynamic picture of the artist here, one that requires endurance and initiative. His portrait doesn't include the glamorous lifestyle of a performance poet who receives accolades or standing ovations. Carlos is imagining an artist who maintains a strong connection with the community whose "fullness" he is constantly trying to represent through performance. Spoken word poetry functions for Carlos as a way to cultivate such a connection with his community, and the usually soft-spoken, jovial jokester is uncompromising in his standpoint on this issue:

> Carlos: It's that way with a lot of rappers that are out there running their mouth. They're not living in the same communities the people listening to them are. They're saying whatever, and they got people, I'm not saying that necessarily it's their fault if like, someone's listening to their album and they decide to shoot someone because they heard it. In a way it's that person's fault because they should have self-control, you should be more responsible for yourself. But at the same time, the rapper should have accountability for what you're saying to the people. Don't just put out all this stuff or this garbage and then when something happens you're like, oh it's not my fault . . . eventually someone's gonna influence somebody, and that's what I hate. Cuz people [rap artists] are out here living in their, in a house, not in the ghetto anymore, not on streets anymore, so they don't care anymore.

For Carlos, social responsibility has a direct connection to individuals "be[ing] more responsible for themselves," so individual responsibility is integral to being committed to a community's development. Carlos is also suggesting that spoken word poetry or performance (in his example, rap music) is a vehicle for a system of checks and balances. The individual should have "self-control" and the rapper "should have accountability for what you're saying to the people." He continues to describe the typical behavior patterns for hip hop music stars who make it big and start earning larger incomes: they move from the ghetto to a suburb, distancing themselves from the very people whom they are supposed to be speaking with and for. Carlos describes these hip hop artists as sellouts because "they're not living in the same communities the people listening to them are" the minute they can afford not to. Upward social mobility is cast in a very negative light in this instance. Carlos is harsh in his judgment of artists who use their newly acquired affluence to pass upward. He describes it as an act of desertion that is the highest form of treason. Whenever the rapper moves out and no longer resides "in the ghetto anymore, not on the streets anymore," for him that automatically demonstrates that the artist "don't care anymore."

The competing desires that surface in Carlos's impassioned monologue touched a tender and sensitive spot for most of the members of Collective Energy. Immediately, everyone began naming famous artists that had acted just the way Carlos described. After some thought, several members also mentioned similar instances that occurred within their own families when a particular family member would "make it" and then either physically move or simply remove themselves from associating with the family who remained poor with limited access to limited options. This point is of interest because of the role that each student artist in Collective Energy played. Let me explain.

While the spoken word and musical performances created and produced by Collective Energy are certainly functional and make an effort to address social issues they perceived as crucial, these performances are also particular to the student artists and their cultural and physical communities at Penn State. By functional, I mean that these student artists have access, ability to perform, and opportunity to engage in and among their communities. The art forms represented in this particular collective are relevant in a very particular moment. The high numbers of the student body in attendance at the programs where Collective Energy performs and the warm reception those students respond with are a form of proof that the performances "offer forth motivation." However, these student artists evolved, as did their styles, interests, needs, and the specific social issues they wished to address. The communities and experiences that link them to "the people" when they first arrived at Penn State may not remain relevant as they grow. Already, their enrollment in higher education is a privilege they enjoy, yet it is separating them from the "oppressed and marginalized communities" Karenga refers to in his theory and that some of the members of Collective Energy call home. This conflict raises particular questions about accountability for the student artists. Does the artwork produced have to be experienced directly by the community, and, if so, how is that to be determined? Also, is it possible for the artist to control how the audience interprets her?

When I raised these questions to the group that night, a heavy silence filled the room. We were each implicated by the desires we harbored and the choices we made. By our very presence on a college campus, we were already labeled as sellouts for making attempts to pass in the way that Carlos had described. Passionate performances that pulled on our deeply personal familial experiences did not excuse us. We were each guilty of striving toward success, even when success meant leaving behind the places that raised us. Our occupation of such conflicted territory stirred Carlos to write. I include an excerpt here from a poem that quickly became his signature piece:

Shooter

Carlos Mason

. . . I may seem like I'm bragging
But it's my words that are arrogant
They can't help it
All they can do is say what they're saying
They can't help the way you felt
Shit
All I know is I got my finger on this trigger
And it's aimed at you, Slick
So when I shoot you better pray you don't get hit
Even I have to face these clips
In the past I ain't been no angel
So best believe if I mess up
I got no problems turning this gun on myself
So if you want me with my hands up
I'll reach for the sky
I'll tell you my demons
Cuz honest is how I want to go when I die . . . I'll tell you the truth
But be careful . . . I'm a shooter so when I speak I'm gonna shoot . . .

. . . When I reach into your pocket it's not to take but to
Give you change
You may be outside my range, but I promise I'll reach you
I know I said earlier I was gonna shoot you, but that's just how I teach you
So remember if I shoot, it's not just to embarrass you
It's because I see something inside of you worth saving too . . .

In this brief soundbite of Carlos's poem, he manages to use spoken word poetry performance to meet several of his needs as a socially responsible artist in the way he defines such a person. Carlos uses "Shooter" to address the issues he brought up in the discussion of Karenga's theory. These issues include individual accountability, his role as a socially responsible artist for his audience, and the ongoing conflict that takes place as a result.

Carlos begins by placing the responsibility first upon his words, giving them the adjective "arrogant" but disclaiming repercussions that may result from that attribute by saying, "They can't help it" because "All they can do is say what they're saying." It's as if his words have a life of their own, as if he is attempting to disengage with the political or social consequences of his words. Yet Carlos almost immediately follows up by implicating himself in the situation, saying "even I have to face these clips," meaning that he is holding himself to the same stringent standard, if not a higher one than he is holding his audience to. He is even willing to offer the personal disclosure that Q insisted was a vital characteristic of a socially responsible artist. Carlos is professing a willingness to "tell you my demons," which exhibits his readiness to participate equally with the audience in the practice of responsibility and accountability. This removes any previous allusion that "Shooter" was a poem aimed only at the crowd, preaching or pointing out the wrong in others—Carlos readily admits to his own mistakes in an effort to lend authenticity and sincerity to his piece. His attempt to become intimate with his audience signals a desire for connection and relatability with them.

Carlos continues to develop his role for the audience by speaking to those members who may be just beyond his reach. When he confesses, "You may be outside my range, but I promise I'll reach you," Carlos bravely owns up to the fact that his spoken word poetry may not reach or relate to every listening ear. By acknowledging this shortcoming and by promising to continue to work in order to grow his reach, Carlos is holding himself accountable by vocalizing this to his audience. Spoken word poetry morphs from a vehicle that simply works to deliver a message into the message itself; Carlos recognizes that the spoken word gives him leave to enter and refuses him access all at once. This disconnect from his audience parallels the distance that arises from his separation from the streets of Philadelphia because of his enrollment at Penn State. By declaring this struggle, he also makes a commitment to continue to work toward that unattainable goal of "representing fullness" that he mentioned earlier. For a student artist like Carlos, such a goal requires attention to his actions on the plane of school and for his membership at home. The work of investigating and navigating the in-between and overlaps of our individual artistic and political identities that began in the Collective Energy workshops extended beyond the realm of artistic creation and motivates border-crossing in other areas of our lives (Gómez-Peña and Sifuentes 2011, 7). Performances that result in mobilization in daily life are the most fundamental and yet transformational experiences of all. Spoken word works to hold Carlos accountable and at the same time permits him to fall short of his goal. Liability and forgiveness are both necessary, because spoken word poetry performance is a process focused on relationship rather than a final product that halts at the drop of the stage curtain.

Carlos ends this portion by reminding his audience that, despite the overarching violence that is described by the title "Shooter" and the analogy of his words to bullets and his poetry to a gun, he is not there to hurt them or himself: for Carlos the socially responsible artist, to harm self *is* to harm the community. Instead he uses this analogy to grab the attention of an audience that is accustomed to hearing young men of color speak of violence. What makes this poem stand out is that his use of images of a reckless gunman asks his audience to utilize a certain amount of accountability for themselves—he isn't going to spell it out for them. As he mentioned in the earlier discussion,

> CARLOS: I'm not saying that necessarily it's their fault if like, someone's listening to their album and they decide to shoot someone because they heard it—in a way it's that person's fault because they should have self-control, you should be more responsible for yourself.

Carlos delivers a disturbing image of violence along with an expectation of his audience's participation in his performance. He expects them to contribute to this exchange of performance by marshalling their own sense of "self-control." He ends by seeking to communicate the value and worth they each possess and to uncover that he "sees something inside of you worth saving too." While salvation may be a large bill to fit for a rising performer, what I want to emphasize is Carlos's recognition of the precious significance that he attributes to the varied audiences that hear his poem. No matter which communities they came from, he used "Shooter" to bury his hands inside their hearts or as Stacey put it, "that deep, deep place," and to command their attention to their own treasure chests. However they are defined, social relationships are the core of social responsibility, and those relations were central to Collective Energy's function and form.

Action research is above all concerned with the production of knowledge and understanding, which is precisely why performances by arts-based groups like Collective Energy make a good fit with this method of research (Carson and Sumara, 1997, xviii). As stated earlier, one of my main focuses for Collective Energy was to provide time and space through the weekly workshop sessions that would allow and encourage members to develop their ideas about the role they, as artists, play in enacting social change. This process requires that we consider audience, self, society, and the message we wish to convey. In order for our original performances to be effective at this task, they must engage with the surrounding community around issues relevant to that community. Thus, the knowledge each performance produces "is always knowledge about one's self and one's relations to particular communities" (xvii). These relationships are understood to be constantly evolving and performed differently depending upon the circumstances and personal context that never stays the same. I asked each student artist to look to the external to better understand the internal effects of their cultural production and vice versa.

Navigating Meaning in the World

Previously, I looked at several examples of moments when spoken word poetry functioned as a form of recognition of self and subjectivity for the student artists in Collective Energy. Often as an art form, spoken word poetry is viewed as a therapeutic practice, a tell-all forum that is cathartic in nature with no rules or standards of excellence. While spoken word and most forms of creative expression often relieve us emotionally and serve as a means to turn inside out the private in public, it is for these very same reasons that I argue there are always repercussions for the language that we use. Therapy is meant to remove the filter of the patient, allowing her to "get things off her chest," while spoken word poetry is a tool for becoming critical of the filter, the patient, and the things. Also, based upon the meaning of artistic social responsibility that was continuously negotiated by Collective Energy, liability must be considered by the artist and the audience for every part of a performance, including language and delivery. From this perspective, spoken word poetry is not a free-for-all, allowing the artist to glide above intersections of performance and accountability for the message in the art; instead it is a critical process of meaning construction. Because of these junctures, spoken word poetry is always political. In these meeting points, its meaning is created not only by the artist but by the audience, who bears witness to the performance as well. In this section, I further explore the ways that spoken word poetry functions as an instrument for the members of Collective Energy as we struggle to navigate and negotiate meaning in the world.

If spoken word poetry and performance are indeed assistants in our attempts at charting a course through the world, we must ask first what did the members of Collective Energy consider as "the world"? More specifically, what did they consider to be their "community"? How did performance stretch or strengthen these definitions? What sorts of landscapes did the group seek to steer through as artists and students? What sorts of landscapes constructed the terrain we discovered during this experience together? How did these discoveries contribute to an awareness of the complex identities and borders that shaped our experience? In the following, I tease apart moments when we worked to make these borders, and thus our world, as acceptable to ourselves as we could while at the same time seeking out alternatives that appeared to offer improvement on the conditions we live in. I quickly found that spoken word poetry, song, and performance offered pockets of peace and cracks of frustration, often simultaneously.

Collaboration and Community

The idea of an artist collective where collaborative performances were developed appealed to me, and forming these collaborations ranked high on my list of goals for Collective Energy as well. Mind you, I had never once written a poem with another poet. The closest work with other artists I had done was in the recording studio, which is different from constructing a performance with another artist. I had zero experience in this area, and that is why it was a goal for me. Group work has always made me nervous. One can never be certain that other members of the group will pull their weight when it comes time to work. Although the assignment appears ironic because of the cooperative structure behind Collective Energy, I was attempting to create an experience based on what I thought was beneficial for those of us involved and was not limited to what I understood how to do. I also wanted to demonstrate that I was engaging in each of the activities that the rest of the members were; I did not hold myself exempt from participating just because of my role as leader/researcher.

Part of my hesitation behind writing a piece with someone else stems from my experiences in traditional classrooms where being silenced or excluded when working with others had been the norm for me. Sometimes my tendency is to overcompensate and be the most dominant leader in a group. I knew that working together and structuring Collective Energy so that we would have to create collaborative pieces would be a learning experience for us all. Not so surprisingly, by the end of the year I had not completed a single poem with another artist in the group, although several of them had paired up and worked together to create new work. However, I drew the conclusion that our hour-long show counted as collaboration because it featured the concurrence of many different perspectives through a cohesive performance. Though the show did offer one conclusion, it was no final answer at all, because it pointed to yet another question: Did this mean that collaboration and collectivity were equivalent to a group consensus or a feeling of unity? In my search for what collaboration and collective work could mean, I turn to Ewa Kuryluk (1994), whose words trouble the ideas behind "collectivity" by insisting "collective standards must be questioned, not confirmed by art, and artists must fight for *autonomy*: their right to explore and express whatever they find important or interesting" (13–14). According to Kuryluk, we are supposed to cultivate and separate individual voices and opinions that manifest in our artwork. She determines that self-representation leads to self-sufficiency, which in turn strengthens any collective made up of artists who do so. Practically speaking, the academy is not always geared toward cultivating a sense of self-efficacy, particularly for artists. From Kuryluk's perspective, participating in a group membership does not mean giving up one's standpoint or specific point of view. Instead, the specificity of an artists' viewpoint is to be valued, even when the expression of such a perception may first appear to disrupt the cohesiveness of the community the artist is joined with. Being a member of a collective in no way abolishes the personal voice; rather, as Linda Alcoff (1995) comments, part of the reward of work that "engages collectively with others" is that "aspects of our own location less obvious to us might be revealed" (112). The very performance of the juxtaposition of our autonomous viewpoints demands that the performers and audience members make space for multiple voices to be heard. When a performance becomes an investigation, new concepts must be envisioned in order to make sense of contradictory positions, and this is how transformation might take place. It is only through a deliberate investment in Kuryluk's (1994) autonomy that an effective collective can begin to be formed. Spoken word poetry functions as an expression of that autonomy as well as a skill that links each member, no matter how diverse in their particular experience. Understanding how community might have been perceived by Collective Energy is the next step in determining how the idea of community was utilized throughout our process together. I asked each member how they defined community, and I focus on responses from Alyssa and Q in the following.

> Alyssa: I have, I have a lot of different . . . I don't . . . that's been one of the things that has been like hard is being able to identify community because I'm . . . I think it's supposed to be one thing, but then you learn that you can have multiple communities and I consider myself have, having multiple art, artistry talent. And I don't know if I've ever actually identified what those are. I know there's like different values within each collective that may affect what art comes out . . . but Collective Energy has provided me with a community that I have not . . . you know how some things are just kind of like meant to go together. Collective Energy is like on a different scale than everything else. For me it's just a little bit more . . . it provides that, that space for critical thinking that people don't want to touch.

Alyssa gestures to the ways that multiple memberships in different communities are often sites of competing values. How does an artist choose which values are priorities? How do these choices impact the type of artwork that is performed? Alyssa also references Collective Energy as a community that "provides space for critical thinking that people don't want to touch." Critical thinking is a necessary part of the process of embracing individual values and exploring the contending values of others who are members of the community. When a strategy for critical thinking practice is taught and then applied from an artistic standpoint, then it can be digested and rehearsed through a performance. The sharing and remixing that result when critical analyses are discussed by a group of people demand several qualities: trust, intimacy, and openness. The stage is not the only place where pedagogy through performance takes place. For Collective Energy, our weekly group meetings were integral to the building of our community, yet these meetings were not without impediments. The meetings were lengthy and took place every Tuesday evening. Toby and I were often exhausted; details and logistics had to be worked out, groceries for each week's dinner had to be bought and prepared. She was completing her dissertation at the same time this program was taking place as well, and I was working for her and enrolled in full-time graduate study myself. In addition to the internal pressure to succeed and produce excellent artwork/performances, I was also realizing how much energy was required to engage the student artists for a sustained period of time in the development workshops. I can remember being shocked at how similar teaching my class was to leading these workshops. Unpredictable. The student artists sometimes came prepared, other times they were distracted, grumpy, or absent. There were workshops full of silence, and at other points we were constantly talking over each other and experiencing multiple unplanned interruptions. To my untrained hand and ear, this cacophony was a *mess.* Part of this anxiety was the fact that I had indeed hand-chosen each of these student artists. What did it say about me if I couldn't keep their attention long enough to coax beautiful turns of phrase from their souls and transform them into spoken word artists of the year? I never felt satisfied with what we came up with, and yet I had never felt more committed. A performer, yes—I had been a performer for years. A teacher though? Me? I felt like a fraud. Here I was with my poor grammar, impulsive decision making, and sensitive as a raw nerve to boot. What was I doing here trying to organize other artists? Teacher was a role I was extremely uncomfortable playing, and it frayed my nerves like an unfinished hem. I was not only learning to navigate the terrain with Collective Energy—they were learning to trust my sense of direction as well.

All of these unpredictable elements of the environment are directly related to the level of vocal participation the student artists would commit to at any given time. bell hooks's (1989) work on the issues of finding voice and community speaks aptly to the difficulties we experienced by interpreting the act of coming to voice as an act of resistance (12). Pulling examples from her own experiences, hooks continues to illustrate what she considers to be the challenges of choosing to speak out from a personal experience that may not be shared by others, even those who stand in "community" with you. She states, "It becomes easy to speak about what the group wants to hear, to describe and define experience in a language compatible with existing images and ways of knowing, constructed within social frameworks that reinforce domination" (14). Here hooks considers the extensive social pressure and training that institutions of education, popular culture, and the media have used to construct the ways in which it is socially acceptable to speak and listen. These constructions do not magically evaporate simply because a community is based around social change. Each member of Collective Energy had to work at relearning what it means to listen and speak from a critical place. Thoughtful time and careful word choice became priorities that were doubly important because of the weight that we all agreed words carry. As poets and songwriters especially, we strove to exercise caution with our words because, as Tony reminded us in his poem, "words have power." To change the way we speak is to alter our lifestyle, and even more substantially, it's about shifting subjectivities. It is always difficult to break a habit, particularly one that we are trained in from childhood. hooks suggests we learn to speak and listen in a new way, and this implies that in doing so, we can reconstruct the social frameworks that form the support structure for domination. This practice is easier said than done.

Alyssa confirmed hooks's suspicion that it takes hard work to maintain a sense of personal integrity even when that means not saying what the group "wants to hear" (14). Alyssa acknowledged that "different values" existed within "each collective that may affect what art comes out" thus also affecting the process by which that art is produced. Group, collective, and community work is perilous. Just as the researcher strives to be aware of all the existing underlying and forming relationships that shape what is being researched, the community member must plot a route through and among relationships and priorities and, as an artist, make a personal decision that affects the greater public. However, the goal here is not to necessarily align every single value of the artist with every value of the community but to provide the space and tools with which to think, communicate, investigate, and explore those values on an analytical level. The work of a community and a collaborative artistic project is to make room for the expression of the ongoing results of those explorations. Ensuring the continuation of this work is a rigorous challenge for even the most experienced researcher or teacher. Constant momentum and a willingness to reexamine and revisit a performance is also a continuing challenge for the budding artist, and so creating spoken word poetry and original songs function as challenge.

Q chimes in here with her view on how participating, performing, and identifying herself within a group like Collective Energy functioned to challenge her.

> Q: Because in all actuality like, like I said, you have a lot of people surrounding you, but everybody is not going to think like you. And not necessarily saying that everybody in Collective Energy agrees with you, but they can challenge your perspective on a different level that makes you either think more by like adding

> to, to your thought or understanding why it may not work all the time. You know what I mean? And sometimes you just need that . . . sometimes you need something off the general level of being in Penn State and this is what I encounter. You know what I mean? And I believe that the people who were willing to participate in that . . . I don't know. There's just something about this group of people that we have now. It's just like they want to be there for the reason of like challenging their minds and, and that's what you need around you sometimes. Like you—and not all the times but that's what people need around them you know.

According to this excerpt of her interview, Q's visions of community involved being challenged by having to "think more" or by asking that another person "understand why it may not work like that all the time." Q also characterizes "willingness" as a way to describe the members of such a community—one that supports you in spite of their objections or oppositions to what you may value. Communication becomes vital for the community as well, so that the contesting viewpoints are productively expressed.

Q also mentions Collective Energy was "off the general level of being in Penn State," and from this statement I deduce that she is referring to the very specific and unaddressed population that, while very small in numbers, Collective Energy was made up of. Q also mentions that the other student artists were "like [her]—and not all the times" meaning that she recognized they shared similar values such as a desire to grow artistically, to do well in school, to speak forthrightly and politically, yet they weren't identical; the shared values weren't necessarily consistent across the board. Two important points surface here. First, Q recognizes that the consistency and "likeness" she shares with her peers is valuable: they are striving toward the same goals. Secondly, and perhaps most interesting of all, Q does not express a need or desire to "necessarily agree with" or assimilate to the other members of the group. This means that Q can appreciate what they share without feeling required to adapt or adjust herself in the areas that mark her as different from everyone else. Her difference does not mark her as an outsider of the community; instead, what Q finds essential is the *challenge* of working in those differences. In fact, the differences excite her. She is pleased because the other members of her community "want to be there for the reason of like challenging their minds." Their commitment to tackling that challenge earns them Q's respect and serves as her connection with them.

It is this same sense of challenge that marked a group like Collective Energy as, in Alyssa's words, a space that "people don't want to touch." When I probed her further, she said she didn't "feel that intellectual connection so much [with others] because they are aware of different things, or aren't aware of things." Alyssa's perspective supports Q's earlier statement that community entails a willingness to enter into conversation and engage with others on an intimate level even when such close contact infers personal discomfort. This sense of connection Alyssa felt as a result of her artistic endeavors with Collective Energy is a point of individual interest, because when I first invited her to join the project, she was excited but there was some apparent hesitation. When I reminded her of that moment during our one-on-one interview, she responded as follows.

> Alyssa: Well as an artist you know it's funny because I don't think I actually always thought of myself as an artist. I guess I did—technically, I was a performing artist. But it never was so visible to me until Collective Energy, I think, when it was like that group of artists like so many different talents, I was just like wow. Like I do have something to give and I think first coming into Collective Energy I was like, you know, what's my place here? I don't even know. I don't really know what I'm supposed to do or what is going to happen. But then finally it just kind of clicked and I just kind of, like, it was probably the beginning . . . of me seeing like through an artist's lens . . .

At first glance, this bit of text may appear as if it belongs in the previous section because it nods to how performance assists Alyssa in recognizing herself as an artist. However, it wasn't until Alyssa performed with a group of artists striving for similar goals but using a variety of tactics that her role as an artist became "so visible" to her. Her participation within the Collective Energy community designated for her "the beginning" of her viewpoint being shaped intentionally through her production of performance art within a context of other artists. Alyssa's location within Collective Energy enabled her to operate in old discourses through a new way.

Jonathan, our only other vocalist, said his community included the place that he "came from" as well as his "audience." When I asked him who his audience was composed of, he told me, "I want my audience to be anybody who will listen." Alyssa repeated Jonathan's reply word for word and extended the thought by saying part of her work as an artist was "to connect to [her] audience." Alyssa and Jonathan's desire to be heard and thus recognized connotes singing as a way to bond with more than one community at a time and therefore be considered a resident of many communities at once. Both Alyssa and Jonathan were using performance as a platform to increase the range of their community; it was a way to expand the numbers of those in membership that could relate to their work and would signify that this relation was so, thus bearing witness to their testimony. As a result, the two singers would also gain admittance to communities to which they would not otherwise be attached, forging "transformative alliances across mythical categories" (Underiner 2000, 1295). Performance then becomes a means to align with parties and people that their other community memberships "distinguish" them from. At the same time, it allows them to separate completely from the parts of society where there is no perceived magnetism or reason to connect. In terms of community, performance provides mobility, or a method of "passing" between and among a mixture of populations. Everything you change also changes you. Community is inevitably modified by performance, molded into something different during each act, fluctuating and unstable, the terrain of meaning that is being negotiated unsettled and resettled with each performance.

The community I intended for Collective Energy to form was distinguished from the surrounding communities of Penn State and the geographical community of central Pennsylvania because of our focus on producing socially responsible performances. The common characteristics and interests that bound each member to the next was an investment in artistic growth. Collective Energy was perceived as distinct by the rest of the student body because it was the only group of its kind on campus that was united centrally by a focus on arts for social action. Framing what counts as community is important in order to better locate the ways that my understandings were complicated and challenged.

I did not factor in the personal expense of being emotionally invested when I began analyzing the people and project I care about so deeply. Part of the power of this topic is its immediate relevance to several of my own communities, and that is also what makes this research moment sobering. My own memberships in several sorts of communities do not protect me from the consequences that may result from belonging in this one. To belong to a community increases the chance that another member of that community may speak or act on my behalf. Representation for me, as a woman of color especially, is a historically dangerous subject. Another person's assumption and action in my place upsets the philosophy that suggests no one person should speak for another. My motive for endeavoring to explicitly link and promote a sense of connection with and among the members of Collective

Energy is by no means absent of selfishness—I clearly wanted it because I thought it would benefit me as well as the group. I quickly abandoned (if I ever attempted it at all) the management of emotion or involvement that most qualitative researchers strive for. Instead, I actively sought out a raw and vulnerable position that did not implicitly equal a significant and meaningful connection with each member of the community that was Collective Energy. However, it was this type of connection that I was on a search to find. I was not the only one. A sense of connection was expressly named by other student artists as a goal.

> Alyssa: And I, I, I always strive to make that connection cause I don't want to ever be a performer on stage that people are just like watching and they're like oh she sounds good. I want to be, I want to be more than that . . . and I feel like it's me on stage and I want people to feel that. I don't want to be distant.
>
> Q: It's like putting yourself out there and taking that risk of being rejected or accepted—
>
> Jonathan: You can, you can see people's intentions shining through even though you know like they, they—it means something to them. So, therefore, it means something to everybody else, you know?

Carlos mentioned his search for connection when he spoke of the socially responsible artist and referenced his home. Stacey and Tony brought it up indirectly whenever they referenced their family stories as starting points for writing. I am bringing it up here, and it is partially a result of a displacement that I felt upon my physical departure from the community that raised and nurtured me prior to my arrival at graduate school. Speaking effectively on behalf of the artist and activist of color that has been isolated from her home community, James Baldwin (1969) suggests that for the artist

> to continue to grow, to remain in touch with herself, she needs the support of that community from which, however, all of the pressures of American life incessantly conspire to remove her. And when she is effectively removed, she falls silent—and the people have lost another hope. (xviii)

The absence of crucial support that Baldwin speaks of was largely felt by me when I moved to this tiny college town. Hope was indeed evaporating until

Toby hired me to work at the PRCC and we developed Collective Energy. When I first met with each student artist to extend the invitation to join Collective Energy, they were excited, not just to have a chance to perform but, as Q put it, "to have a sort of artsy family." I was both relieved that I was not the only person having this intensely lonely time and disturbed that so many of my students and peers expressed this destabilizing sensation of unbelonging and isolation while at school and then again upon their return to their home communities.

There are few cultural venues where we live and hardly any formal conversations about the effect this has on student artists. There were no initiatives resembling Collective Energy that worked toward effectively fostering artistic and socially minded development on our campus. There is a certain cost and sacrifice involved in choosing to pursue higher education that seems to require this division—the new competition of our home communities with our unfamiliar academic space. In our one-on-one interviews, I also asked each student artist what she or he felt was the best aspect of the Collective Energy experience. Five out of six of the members said that it was the weekly group meetings. I was floored. These three-hour meetings were the source of so much complaining during the course of the year that I did not know what to do. Everyone was exhausted at the end of each meeting and couldn't wait to depart, their minds already filled with the tasks they had yet to complete before the night was out. Cell phones vibrated incessantly during our meetings and almost drove me crazy. What I found at the end of the year was that these same obligatory but very regular meetings were the crucial core of the community building that took place during Collective Energy. It was not only the product of our performances but the process of our rehearsal that knit together the bond of our group that may otherwise seem random and uncoordinated. There was a discipline centering our commitment to those three hours each week, sharing them jealously with one another and devoted solely to what we were building together as Collective Energy. It was like an amateur wrestling match—uncoordinated, each opponent skilled and trained, but not choreographed—between discipline and desire. Desire to be a better artist, to be a better friend, to be together in this camaraderie that we had never experienced before, but it was not always pleasant nor did we always want to exercise. Sometimes the desire was the exercise, the discipline. In the wrestling match it grew increasingly difficult to see which was which and who was winning.

I have also found the term "community" is often used interchangeably with the word "collective" in reference to a group of people who work together or who "represent" a certain demographic. For the purposes of this study and as a basic definition of community, I view it as "a group sharing common characteristics, goals, or interests and perceived or perceiving itself as distinct in some respect from the larger society within which it exists" (dictionary.com). It was obvious to us that we were different from most of the surrounding campus in which we operated. And this community building, while certainly necessary and beneficial, is not without its traps.

It is often said that one can still be lonely even when one is not alone; this proverb succinctly describes a catch in my plan for Collective Energy that I overlooked as I continued to reorganize the experience. Both of our singers, Jonathan and Alyssa, expressed a feeling of being out of place in their evaluation of Collective Energy. During the year, they may have hinted at their detachment from the community I was so intent upon building; however, neither of them spoke up very adamantly until their interviews at the conclusion of the program. The first time I really observed this crack in the composure of our community was one night during a group meeting when Tony, Carlos, and Jonathan first shared their collaborative effort. They were the first to debut their collab, and the content of the song and the dialogue that followed made me realize what was happening:

CRYSTAL: Soooo, how did the collab work go?

TONY: [speaking directly into the camera] Jonathan is the one that syssed [slang: to hype or brag about] it all up—

TOBY: Mmhmm! Whatever!

CARLOS: Miss 3 a.m. in the morning and giving me the wrong number—

STACEY: What did *I* do?

[There is struggle with setting up Jonathan's keyboard.]

CRYSTAL: Can ya'll set up silently?

Q: Crys, that girl in class was crying for no reason . . .

STACEY: I didn't mean to laugh at her—

JONATHAN: Okay, we ready with the hot collab! The collab of the century!

Tony: We got this together in an hour—

Q: Don't make excuses!

Crystal: No disclaimers!

Toby: Don't be disclaiming it—

Jonathan: We don't even have a beginning . . .

Carlos: Yeah, it's really only half a song—

Jonathan: Hold up, let me turn the beat on—

[The whole exchange has been had in a joking atmosphere, and there is even more laughter as Jonathan turns on the pre-programmed beat to keep time on his keyboard. The sounds of the tinny bass trying be taken seriously couldn't be more comedic in their timing. Jonathan begins to play the chords of the song over the rhythm and it catches the group's enthusiasm.]

Jonathan: [counting off] 1 and 2, 3 and 4

Carlos: [reading from his notebook] One of ya'll got my lyrics . . .

[The group erupts with "Ooooohhhs!" and exclamations of "What!!" because Stacey had mentioned this idea for a poem during an interlude while we were all talking the week before. Everyone immediately recognized the use and metamorphosis of her idea and was excited to hear the outcome. This moment was truly exciting; not only were the fellas working together to produce some music, but they had also incorporated and thus paid homage to Stacey's idea. Eventually, another of Stacey's lines became the official call and response for Collective Energy. There was an ongoing joke that if any of the student artists had writer's block they would simply "borrow" one of Stacey's lines and start their own piece. On the other hand, there is something interesting around gender taking place, because all of the male members of the group used Stacey's idea for their own piece. She seemed pleased that they used it and still wrote her own poem with the line included; however, issues of ownership and silencing might need to be addressed. It is also ironic because the line they borrowed was "one of ya'll got my lyrics," and in this case, all three of the males literally had Stacey's lyric.]

Fly Away (an excerpt)

Lyrics: Jonathan, Tony, Stacey, and Carlos
Music: Jonathan

Carlos: One of ya'll got my lyrics, I said one of ya'll got my lyrics
So why doesn't anyone speak to me
Nothing speaks to me anymore so neither do I
I look for sound waves that can change my brain
waves and help me see light waves to help light
the way

Jonathan: [singing] Lately my mind is wrapped up in deep contemplation
Is this a dream or is this my imagination
I'm using maps for words that lead to no location
Struggling inside my mind to find articulation
Trying to find my voice, when all I can hear is yours
Who I really am is lost inside of your discourse
Is it you or is it me who's really in control
Swimming in your oceans I can't find my shore
Words give me wings to fly
Metaphorical carpet rides
I don't get away, my lyrics will die

Chorus: Ready to fly away, ready to fly away
Ready to fly away from here [2x]

Tony: I will find my way
Nothing more that you can say
I'm writing my own words now, grabbing ownership of
my own lyrics now
Piecing words to melodies just so my soul can hear it now
So no more ghost writers or behind the scenes song biters
No more fixed battles or paid prizefighters
All bets are on me and I got the best odds
It's something like all of them against me
[singing] Asking for lyrics to cover me and sheets of music
become armor for my body

	So I dare you to hit me Punch me and play notes on my chin Squeeze my treble clef and strangle my violin But no matter the number of lashes, my lyrics remain despite the number of bashes So you can sit there as I fly away and watch my dust to dust and ashes to ashes
Jonathan:	Lately my mind is wrapped up in deep contemplation Is this a dream or is this my imagination I'm using maps for words that lead to no location Struggling inside my mind to find articulation Trying to find my voice, when all I can hear is yours Who I really am is lost inside of your discourse Is it you or is it me who's really in control Swimming in your oceans I can't find my shore Words give me wings to fly Metaphorical carpet rides If I don't get away, my lyrics will die
Chorus:	Ready to fly away, ready to fly away Ready to fly away from here [2x]

[The group erupts with wild applause at the boys' performance. General questions such as "how long did it take you?" and comments of "that was so great!" are overlapping so much so that they are not discernable.]

TONY: It was an interesting process 'cause I was all hype like, "Let's do it!" and we were sitting at Jonathan's house, and he was like, "Sooooo . . . ," and then he just started playing and then I don't know, it just—

CARLOS: We just started writing separately and then—

TONY: They all seemed to match—

CARLOS: Yeah—

JONATHAN: Eh . . .

Jonathan's attitude about the working process and rough draft of the collaboration was interesting to note. Knowing him as a perfectionist and a very talented individual led me to believe that those were the causes of his frustration with the initial challenge of working with other artists. I made a mental note to inquire about what it was like for them to work with other writers—as I said before, I had little experience with this area myself. However, as I began to think about it and even question him regarding the most rewarding and challenging moments of the experience, his responses were mixed. I couldn't quite nail down what the expectation was surrounding collaboration. During the discussion that Tony, Carlos, and Jonathan had with us the day they previewed their song, they registered surprise at how smoothly their piece had come together. They seemed to agree that their individual writing "all seemed to match" and naturalized the way that the lyrics complemented the music Jonathan was composing. Their surprise at how "natural" the process seemed struck me because it was contrary to what I had experienced while working with others, particularly when it came to developing performance that tends to be sensitive and very personal for most artists. While the process was roundly seconded by Tony and Carlos, all Jonathan responded with was an uncertain "Eh . . ." At first I chalked this attitude of nonchalant discontent with the fact that he was a new songwriter and perhaps lacked confidence in his work, even though his performances always provoked an impressed response from his audience. When I asked him to describe for me what Collective Energy was in his one-on-one interview he said,

> JONATHAN: Collective Energy, what is it? It's a, it's a group of artists I would suppose for the most part social justice minded in some sense. Socially, socially conscious, I guess we could say. Just, yeah just a group of artists who get together and do stuff—perform for the people. Spoken word. There are a couple of us that sing that's you're kind of lost in the mix sometimes.
>
> CRYSTAL: That's a good way to put it. That's a nice way to put it. What, okay so how do you fit into that would you say?
>
> JONATHAN: I don't know. I wonder about that a lot actually 'cause I don't know if I do fit into that. And you and Toby assured me that I do somehow. But I'm not . . . I don't know cause I really just think of myself as a singer.

Getting "lost in the mix" and not knowing "if I do fit into that" because he thought of himself "just . . . as a singer" were troubling thoughts for me to hear at the end of the year. I was disturbed for two reasons, the first being that I hadn't paid enough attention to Jonathan's experience over the course of the program. I was concerned that he had somehow been neglected or denied some aspect of the experience due to my own oversight. Underneath that layer lay the central issue: What had Jonathan been expecting to gain from this experience? It was clear that performance had functioned for him as a tool of recognition of himself "just . . . as a singer" and as a means to navigate his world. However, it is what his world consisted of that draws my focus. If Jonathan only felt included during certain parts of Collective Energy, what was the difference? How was I to know or to measure those moments, and how could I endeavor to increase their occurrence? At the same time, I consider questions about the student artists taking responsibility for their own experience by understanding that what they sowed in effort and energy was what they would reap. The isolation that Baldwin warned of was still happening in the hallowed space of "community" and in moments of collaboration in spite of our efforts.

As a matter of fact, Jonathan registered surprise about the reactions that his performance incited. When I questioned him about his motivation for music, he said, "Singing just makes me happy . . . I just love . . . I love to sing. I love performing," and he was content to leave his answer at that. When I asked him about a connection with his audience, Jonathan seemed baffled by the way that the crowd would respond to him.

> Jonathan: I don't know. I mean I don't know. I go back and forth between whether I think I'm good and . . . I don't know. Sometimes I think I'm good, sometimes I think I think I'm not. A lot of times I probably think I'm not. So I get up, sing and I'll just, I'll just be praying like Lord don't let me forget no words. I mean just do all right and like everybody is singing and people are like saying that's the most amazing thing they ever heard or anything. A couple of people have told me they cried, which I didn't believe. But they reiterated it so much that I don't know, maybe they weren't lying. I don't know. That boggles my mind cause I don't know. I never cried over anybody singing. Maybe I haven't heard the right person. But so it's just . . . it's kind of weird. Like I get, I get kind of taken aback when people say things like that.

While connection with his audience wasn't a focus, I couldn't figure out why he seemed unhappy with the collaboration or the connection with the other members of Collective Energy. Particularly because his response in the one-on-one interview emphasized that his favorite part was the group meetings as well.

> CRYSTAL: So what was your favorite . . . what do you think was your favorite about Collective Energy? Or your favorite part of, of the experience?
>
> JONATHAN: Being oh I just think it was being around people who loved doing that type of stuff too with like performing or writing or, or anything like that—any aspect of the art, I just love doing it, and that kind of motivates you to do it too. And then we had meetings all the time, so we were like it made me like do stuff. Like it made me like write a little more, think about music a little more than I think about it. And so I, I don't know, I just like that—the consistency of it.

In retrospect for Jonathan, he seemed to appreciate the challenge that Q insisted was a part of what it means to participate in a community membership. His affinity for "consistency" in this particular vocal response again caught me off guard. After more thought, I realized that it was *my* expectation for a certain type of reply or affirmation during the year that made me doubt his full engagement with the process. While Jonathan's feelings of being on the margins of Collective Energy weren't expressed during the experience so that I could address them as the program coordinator, I was frustrated by what I perceived to be his lack of involvement or interest. What I mistook for detachment and a lack of thoughtfulness was really Jonathan wanting to learn but resisting any demonstration of that desire. For him, attendance at the meetings and completion of new songs *was* active involvement—he saw no need to articulate that to me. His actions were what I should have paid attention to, but I was busy trying to figure out what I was doing wrong because he wasn't responding the way I thought he should. Or perhaps I did achieve my goal and *he* simply remained frustrated. Jonathan did not respond with much verbal input, and he didn't vocalize his input during the workshop meetings. However, he attended every single Collective Energy workshop and meeting. He also continued to write original songs, which was a task he had completed only once prior to joining the group. Jonathan also created and cultivated opportunities for solo performances outside of Collective Energy that took place only because of his performances with our group.

Jonathan found Collective Energy to be a home base of sorts—as a space to refuel and recharge. It provided the support that a community is expected to provide and yet freed him to participate at his discretion. Jonathan joined the group during his first year in graduate school and during his first year at Penn State. I posit that he used what he learned in Collective Energy to begin to identify himself as he navigated campus and worked to understand himself as a person and as an artist. It is precisely because participating and holding membership in a community meant something so different to Jonathan that he was invaluable to us all during this experience. Jonathan's proficient talent and stubborn refusal to do anything that he didn't enjoy was a lesson on having a commitment to himself that was a priority even while maintaining an active concern for the broader community. Interestingly enough, when I asked what he wanted to see more of in order to improve Collective Energy, Jonathan mentioned more emphasis on collaboration and more group meetings. The lesson to be learned here is that community building takes a variety of autonomous forms. Performance can function as a way to build community in ways that cannot be measured or predicted, and often does.

Social change and transformation can only be as effective as the relationships that are formed during the process of building community. For the student artists of Collective Energy, those relationships were forged during the rehearsal and workshop meetings where we learned that envisioning ourselves as artists allows us to enact what we conceive. Through an exploration of Q and Carlos's ideas about what it means to be socially responsible, it's clear that the Collective Energy experience taught us about the context of our performances. We had to have a foundational grasp of how our external context impacted our performance content and how that content might then disrupt our immediate context. Defining and developing community among ourselves helped us to better understand the challenges and invitations that social responsibility might offer us as artists. It was through our relationships with one another that we gained the courage to act against and reimagine the things that bound us. Examining the behind-the-scenes process of development for socially responsible performances, the workshop content, and the unique perspectives of the group members as they experienced Collective Energy offers the opportunity to trace the roots of a powerful product and end performance.

3

When the Audience Claps Back

Like any new teacher, when I first stood in front of a class I was excited and idealistic, sure that I could change the world through these students—and equally sure that they needed to be changed. As a spoken word artist, I never viewed my audience that way. My perspective of my own position as a teacher and as an artist determined how I interacted with each of my audiences. Looking back, it strikes me as ironic that my first semester teaching was also my first semester working with Collective Energy. After that first fifteen weeks, I realized that the most important skill I could cultivate to improve in both arenas was the ability to *listen.* That it was not enough to trust my performances or my lectures to simply transmit cultural values, memory, and identity to my students or my audience (Gómez-Peña and Sifuentes 2011, 5). I needed to be much more intentional about the transaction that was happening in my classroom and on the stage. In an effort to do so, I invited students from a class I was teaching to attend our on-campus open mic cultural program.

I knew that since Collective Energy was performing as the feature for the open mic, the students from my class would be guaranteed a quality arts and culture experience with conscious material. I was also excited because I hoped to connect the inner workings of this small, integrated arts group to the larger context in which they carried out a majority of their daily activity. I was expecting positive feedback from my class, anticipating their "teachable moments" to occur as they connected to the issues of class, race, and inclusion that I kept attempting to raise in our discussions. I was also expecting that the members of Collective Energy would finally begin to view themselves as taking up the role of artist activists—the politicized and energized embodiment of social change. I was in for a double dose of surprise.

Bed: A Spoken Word Lounge

One of the primary outlets for the performances of Collective Energy was a spoken word program designed as part of my duty as an event programmer at the cultural center on campus. This program was titled Bed: A Spoken Word Lounge. As the only consistently supported open mic on Penn State's University Park campus, the Bed cultural initiative was created to provide an opportunity for students to perform and showcase various art forms with an emphasis on spoken word poetry. Students who arrived late were often turned away at the door. While the program was marketed for all students and faculty/staff at the university, constituents often identified with communities of color; most of the students are African American, Latino, Asian, or any combination of the three.

To put this in perspective, consider that the campus we lived on is a predominantly White institution where enrollment exceeds forty thousand; however, students of color comprise only 12.9 percent of that student body. Needless to say, there are classes where only one, two, or no students of color are enrolled. Transitioning to a large-scale campus where there is a fresh history of racial tension and violence proves difficult and unfortunately dangerous for many of the students. Many of the students of color have moved from an urban setting to a rural town where many of the population have never had any personal interaction with a person of color. The PRCC's main function is to provide spaces for cultural education, engagement, and development, and that is why the spoken word lounge program Bed, was created.

Most of the student artists outside of Collective Energy that sign up to perform on the open mic at Bed are student artists of color. However, anyone present is welcome to participate. Collective Energy served as featured performers at each of the Bed programs held during the semester. The content of their songs, poetry, and monologues were uncensored, raw, and often center on themes of racism, the results of growing up in poverty, social injustice, and love gone graphically right and wrong. The performances were intense in delivery, though the styles ranged from slam poetry, to ballads being accompanied by the piano, to pieces that were read calmly while sitting on a stool.

The open mic represented to these student artists an opportunity to voice their discontent with their current surroundings and environment, a chance to declare how they see themselves and their roles despite images portrayed by history books or popular culture. The opportunity for creative expression surrounding social justice issues is also particularly salient as there is a tense history of racial conflict on our campus. The tumultuous atmosphere has resulted in violence against students of color, vandalism, and even threats of death. I am not suggesting that a single cultural program, even one as fantastic and necessary as Bed, will miraculously dissipate racial tension, but what it did is allow a space to create and recreate cultural meanings, making difference and friction visible and therefore recognizable and requiring that everyone present contribute and extract, becoming aware of their choices. Bed was a stage and opportunity for Collective Energy to do just that every time we performed as headliners at the end of the open mic session.

Jennifer Drake (2002) addresses the tension that inevitably arises in any sort of pedagogy or art by asking artists and audiences "to understand how both images and words contribute to oppressive and/or liberating construction of self and other" (215). The fact of the matter is that the images and words used are not necessarily going to be emancipatory for all audience members or students. Realistically, this partnership between audience and performer, or students and teacher, is not a dependable, steady relation. The balance of equality in a performance and classroom setting is uneasy and tilts off balance in a matter of seconds. Power relations shift, as do discourses, and while unstable and precarious, it should not be surprising. While the audience and the performer are both exposed to the ethics and creeds of others, the interpretation of those values is dependent upon the subject positions that individuals inhabit within the community discourses constituted by those in attendance. This exposure is provoking in a challenging and powerful way. New definitions or consequences of decisions that maintaining privilege has may be brought to light, but there is no guarantee that such tactics will be taken up by the audience, nor is this process of performance safe. Meaning and recognition are still bargained for during performance pedagogy, no matter how sound the foundation of internal agency and activity may be. The attempt to make visible those alternate meanings sets the stage for a competition with the discourses that have legacies of privilege invested in the maintenance of oppressive categories and conditions. Such territory is not ceded willingly or quickly.

During my first teaching experience as a graduate student, I was an instructor in the Language and Literacy Education (LLED) block, where my main duty was to teach language arts methods to preservice teachers. My section was the writing emphasis, which means that most assignments and readings focus on how to teach elementary school students how to write. In the meantime, we discussed context, intertextuality, and the ways that our own beliefs and values shape our classrooms. My students are generally at a level equivalent to a junior in their undergraduate studies. I thought it would be a great practical application of what we were learning in the classroom if I offered extra credit to my LLED students if they attended Bed: A Spoken Word Lounge. To provide more specific context for my classroom, I was the only identified person of color and occupied the position of authority in that space. Thus, I was often asked by my LLED students to speak on issues of diversity both inside and outside of the classroom context.

I quickly grew tired of being the point person and contact these students had with a person outside of their own socioeconomic and racial positions. I also realized how many of them had never attended a cultural program because they did not think the programs applied to them personally. They saw no reason or benefit to participate in such events since they were the majority on campus. As a remedy, I extended the invitation to Bed as a means of earning extra credit and asked that they reflect on their experiences as audience members. Eager for extra credit points, many of my students attended the program and responded with mixed feelings. After I received their initial reactions and had several class discussions centered on the issues that they raised, I became conscious of the effects of the performances from Bed—my LLED students were being effectively taught about important social and cultural issues through the performances of their peers.

Several students from my LLED course who attended Bed were deeply disturbed by the performances that they saw. While the lineup of performances was one I interpreted as full of frustration with injustice and unequal power relations yet in no way extraordinary in content, my White students viewed them as a series of hostile personal attacks. One LLED student wrote in her reflection, "I feel like there was just so much hate in there. Why would you make us go to an event like that, where we were the only white people and everybody is mad at us? All of the yelling and anger made me uncomfortable." Her brief experience of discomfort at being the "minority" at a program is a part of the daily lives of the students of color on this campus. Ostracized based on skin color, feeling frustrated because she felt she had no chance to defend herself from what she interpreted as a very personal accusation, gave her the experience of a brief moment that the students of color on campus lived with every day. This student's self-conscious reaction stated that "everybody was mad at us," which shows that her experience was destabilizing at best. Indeed, another student shared that she "didn't realize it was going to be so cultural. I kind of felt like the minority for once, and it really made me think about things." I was perturbed by her reflection because of what she implied by stating that she felt the event was "so cultural." Did she mean that she didn't realize that there were actually going to be real live Black people in the room? And that they would be speaking articulately and demonstrating impressive artistic talent? This LLED student said that attending Bed made her "think about things," but I was worried about her thought process. I had imagined a different conversation that could open up in our class, one that might ask them to reconsider their privilege and position and the values they hold on to. Instead, some of the LLED students thought they could claim to understand and relate to the dangerous lived experiences students of color faced in our small town. Some of the LLED students thought that because they spent two hours in a "cultural program" and experienced some discomfort that probably evaporated shortly afterward, they were suddenly endowed with the ability to intelligently analyze and relate to racial discrimination. Reading their responses, my stomach started to clench. What exactly had I done? In my attempt to educate my LLED class by virtue of exposure through the arts, I had failed them and at the same time invited even more critique aimed at my student artists in Collective Energy. All of this took place in what was designed to be a space of safety. What had I done, indeed.

While I understood the performance to entail an active participatory experience, my LLED students were unprepared to engage with the performers on stage. They had arrived that evening expecting to be entertained in a hands-off sort of way in which they had no investments, no requirements with the exception of their presence. They did not expect to be implicated in any way. The reason for these negative reactions was due in part to the fact that active participation had been demanded of them, and they participated in a performance that was powerful because of its insistence on immediacy and involvement (Denzin 2003, 8). These LLED students were trained through years of school and cinema and traditional theater performance to be spectators in the way that Laura Mulvey (1975) describes them, being allowed a comfortable distance, a "sense of separation" from whatever was taking place on the stage (8). They expected the polite onlooker etiquette to suffice that night at Bed and desired nothing more than the typical experience that provides the "spectator an illusion of looking in on a private world" (8). The illusion was not to be entertained that evening. Suddenly the "private world" that may have amused them but did not *concern* or *involve* them before Bed implicated their sense of responsibility on a very basic level.

The LLED students were responding to a performance that Freire and Macedo (1993) define as a form of pedagogy where the oppressed make a commitment to reveal their oppression and share citizenship in that oppression with their audience (54). The LLED students did not want to share in that citizenship. In fact, they were angry that they were expected to consider life and language as another might experience it. Another student wrote:

> I have never experienced anything like this before. I felt uneasy as I left, like I had just been somewhere I didn't belong. I felt

> like I was unwanted, even disliked by a large group of people, but they didn't even know me. It was a learning experience for me though. I did not realize that people I thought were so alike were actually so different. I grew up in a small white middle class town. I don't have a lot of experience of having to interact with people that are not just like me. I don't think I judge anyone who is not like me, but I have not gone out of my way to try and understand them. This is something I will try to do in the future . . .

Their subject positions had been altered, and the power that was invisible to them prior to this experience was suddenly made very plain as it was removed from them and examined in a public setting. They had been sized up and assigned a membership, and they were uncomfortable with the fit. It came as a surprise when they discovered that as audience members attending Bed, they could not be only passive receptacles of whatever performance takes place on stage; instead, "they engage in a spoken word performance and become part of the performance event" (Denzin 2003, 41). By attending an event such as Bed, these LLED students were committing to acting in a performance of their own. Just as students in a classroom construct a classroom culture, when these same students became the audience members at Bed, they voluntarily accepted the responsibility of their role as audience. This role includes:

> audience to each other's performance, witnesses to the experiences reported upon in the story, as therapists and emotional supporters of the storyteller, as cultural critics commenting on the events that produced the story, and as narrative analysts of the systems of discourse embedded in the narrative. (Langellier in Denzin 2003, 42)

But many LLED students rejected this employment. So what happens when students would rather maintain the deceptively detached gaze of the spectator despite its unhealthy and unhelpful effects on their experience at a performance? Their resistance was not only a rejection of the position of an active audience member; according to their reflections it was related to race.

I came to understand that the transformative power of performance was not a "feel-good" time for the students from whom the power was shifting. Ill-equipped to morph from spectator to participatory audience member, much less understand what was happening, the students resisted. Loudly.

This resistance is not uncommon, according to Jyl Lynn Felman (2001); in fact, she warns of the often violent reaction of students who are unprepared to give up the role they are accustomed to playing. Felman (2001) says that during a performance "a new location of aesthetic excellence and social concern" must be jointly discovered by the performer and the audience member (22). And although I knew that performance pedagogy was supposed to propel "both parties . . . to someplace different," I wasn't sure what to do when that destination wasn't agreed upon. I was less sure what to do when the new location confronted me with a classroom divided.

At that point, the classroom, much like the performance space, was a construction zone. Norman K. Denzin (2003) considers performance art pedagogy as something that "happens when conditions of identity construction are made problematic and located in concrete history. . . . in this moment, performers claim a positive utopian space where a politics of hope is imagined" (17). The space that the performers claimed contradicted the boundaries that the audience members thought they had a right to occupy with minimum disturbance. I realized that the competing discourses that sounded so good on paper were unsteady terrain to navigate. It seemed difficult for the LLED students to grasp the idea that perhaps there was something useful and solid in the multiplicity of perspectives that they shared when challenged with the possibilities the performers expressed that night.

I tried to explain to these students that performance art vested toward social justice, and my own insistence that they read and discuss the work of students of color and their experiences was not asking them to give up how they name themselves—only that they remember how others are naming them in the discourses that they share, or perhaps don't share. In other words, we all play a multitude of roles whether we accept the positions or not. I wanted these students to understand how "race, class, and gender oppressions limit human agency and the freedom that individuals have to act in given ways" (Denzin 2003, 228). I also wanted them to understand how spoken word and performance are forms of agency. When they practice this art form, whether by performing or becoming participatory audience members, they have the chance to imagine new possibilities for their futures and new ways to interpret history, beginning with their own. I saw evidence of this every time a classroom conversation broadened to include another cultural or socioeconomic perspective that was not represented in the classroom. I sometimes noticed students paying closer attention to the language they chose during a discussion. There were always those few who continue to attend cultural events on campus, even when not being persuaded by the lure of extra credit.

Performance enables social change because the reflexive critiques that take place during and after performance also make room for the imagination and enactment of new identities and cultural practices that explode oppressive historical dictates regarding cultural identity. In the case of my LLED class, the critical discussion we shared after the performance was the space in which they were able to sort out how spoken word poetry can be a powerful agent of change. As for the student artists, their response was somewhat different. In the midst of their performance, they were experiencing what Mulvey (1975) describes as the "thrill of leaving the past behind without rejecting it, transcending outworn or oppressive forms, or daring to break with normal pleasurable expectations in order to conceive a new language" (8). This transformation is exciting and all the more satisfying when the student artist and audience member are able to acknowledge what is taking place as a result of their actions and reactions to one another's performance. While my LLED classroom was in turmoil, the Collective Energy meetings were filled with a different type of energy, because the student artists recognized their work had an impact on their audience.

The space Collective Energy created through our weekly workshops and seminars was designed to allow the student artists to become the focal points and to bring their personal knowledge and experiences to the forefront. Our aim was to familiarize them with the tools of performance they could use to become visible and to illustrate social issues they deemed important. Performance of their original art was a method for these student artists to be seen and heard in a climate that worked to mute them, erase their differences, and so disarm them. Choosing to perform in public was dangerous for the student artists, because in so doing, they embodied the controversial issues they addressed, thus taking the risk of becoming a target for criticism at least. While the spaces created for the performances of Collective Energy were considered "safe," they were always socially and politically constructed and were not free from the repercussions of those dynamics. It is also important to remember that being visible or being heard is not always an available choice for student artists, particularly to student artists of color or those who name themselves as allies of the disenfranchised.

I juxtapose these ideas of visibility and access within a chapter focused on activism in order to forthrightly declare a deep appreciation for the multitude of locations and levels of activism that can take place. One type of activism is not necessarily more valuable than another. Oftentimes the quiet methods of resistance that take place subtly in daily routines are the birthing place for the creative ways that activism can be performed purposefully and publicly. The "underground culture" often generates the bravery required for individual public action because it provides a network of support. Throughout the Collective Energy experience, particularly during the initial performances, we were continually asking ourselves: What are the consequences of activism when it requires that the "underground survival cultures" that are often performed in daily tasks and routines be made public and visible? What is at risk when these underground cultures are exposed to the general public? In this way, performance art functioned as a method of renegotiation of the world, attempting to motivate a different action or reaction from a sometimes unwilling audience around an issue or concern they may not be aware of or may not affect them directly. Once again, questions of recognition and visibility circled high above our idealist heads like lazy vultures in the heat of the desert. The student artists responded in a variety of ways to the idea of activism and demonstrated those responses through their performance.

I want to point out that the translation of their performances into the view of the public did not require the student artists to give up or deny the private and subaltern spaces we created during the workshops. In fact, through the small, closed group meetings, and rehearsals we had on a regular basis, these subaltern spaces were maintained and cultivated along with the public performance events. Collective Energy allowed student artists a chance to become visible while simultaneously providing and nurturing their development in a secure environment. Our workshops were our private safe space. A portion of the initial schedule for Collective Energy read very much like a syllabus:

> Our space—including the classroom, rehearsal space, and performance space—will be a safe space. This means that trust is of the utmost importance. We are here to work together and to grow together. As performance artists, each of you knows how it feels to expose your story or risk a piece of your soul on the chance that it will transform at least you if not your audience. An integral part of growing the trust between each of us is your dedication as it manifests itself in attendance. We define attendance as being *present* both in body and mind. Being present means coming prepared to our sessions.

At the start of the program, each student artist was given a copy of the schedule with the expectations for being a member. We eventually shortened this mention of safe space and would remind and reassure one another throughout the process with our adaptation of the infamous

Las Vegas slogan: "What goes on in Collective Energy, *stays* in Collective Energy!" We understood that part of the trust we built was founded on an explicit agreement to maintain confidentiality, not only about the content of the pieces being developed but about the development process. One of the most vulnerable experiences an artist can have is to share work that is not yet "finished." The weekly meetings also provided time and attention for the group to process their performances. This component of the meetings was vital to the beneficial effects and the learning process by each member involved. Collective Energy is a cultural program that intentionally communicated the deliberate inclusion of both the intimate and revealing performance experiences for the specific purposes that such experiences served. Thus, the student artists learned to value both spaces. The overall Collective Energy experience became a demonstration that it is equally crucial to engage in deep reflection and decompressing as well as a public performance event or experience.

By taking advantage of the performance opportunities Toby and I created for them, the student artists had a chance to be "seen" and "heard" and could potentially reverse the ways they were socially trained to view themselves as feeble, incompetent, or illegitimate cultural producers. On the other hand, being visible assumes that one is "knowable" or "recognizable" by others. There is an external versus internal dichotomy that is implicated through a discussion of what counts as visible and invisible. While there are clearly different indications of what is considered external and what is considered internal, to set them up as binaries is a mistake. In the search to be recognized as a viable subject, and thus to be taken seriously, the student artist again battles with issues of representation (see Butler 1993). What happens if the visible does not fairly represent the invisible? Can there be a guarantee that what is made visible will be duly and justly recognized by others? Since performance draws on the contributions of both performer and audience member, this means that the identity of the artist is also negotiated by the audience member and vice versa. The possibilities for recognizing the visible and invisible or the external and internal subject are bargained for by both the self and the outsider. How do these concepts of visibility and voice affect the way that activism is understood? How are these categories of visible and invisible manufactured and maintained and to what end? What is at stake when an artist claims to be an activist? In what ways did Collective Energy's performances disrupt and resist or reproduce these limited subject recognitions?

Coming to recognize the self as a subject can produce unconventional strategies for defying the systems of meaning that work to encase through limitations of subjectivity. Performance then offers a way to showcase or teach those internally based conceptualized strategies to an external audience that may consist of stakeholders in the very status quo that the artist seeks to turn on its head. Collective Energy's hostile campus environment combines with the content of the performances in such a way that "the different patterns of action represent not chance occurrence but the sincere, visual expression of the ideology and psychology of the participants" (Boal 1979, 137). Boal's quote addresses the relations that exist between audience member and artist but shouldn't be misread as though the exchange consists only of a smooth absorption of an intended message deposited neatly from artist to audience and back again. Most folks are passionately and materially invested in their personal and political ideologies. This can make their "sincere expression" a very concentrated and heated exchange. However, once this ideology is translated physically in a visible way that the artist and audience can feel, see, and hear, there is the possibility for them to critically examine their ideas as represented through performance. The physical translation and performance of their beliefs and values also exposes them to the varied and diverse interpretations of those same texts by their peers.

Activism and the Audience

Nina Felshin (1995) offers the following definition for activist art: "This cultural form is the culmination of a democratic urge to give voice and visibility to the disenfranchised and to connect art to a wider audience" (10). Her suggestions on ways to connect with a "wider audience" include making "innovative uses of public space to address issues of sociopolitical and cultural significance and to encourage community or public participation as a means of effecting social change" (9). Felshin's ideas support the belief that art should be accessible and public. What I find interesting is that the role of the audience or the way in which the audience receives the work of the students is not referred to in her definition. In addition, I was curious to note whether or not the student artists would view themselves as activists, and, if so, how did *they* define activism? In our one-on-one interview, Alyssa shared her insight.

> Alyssa: I don't like, I don't like definitions cuz I, like, cause maybe activism to me right now is one thing, but I feel like later on it's going to be something else.

Crystal: Sure. And it should.

Alyssa: Yeah. But for me right now activism is like Q, you know let's do it. And that's . . . cause here I've been like in the classroom studying theory, theory, theory, and I've just like wanted to be like okay now let's act. Theory to practice is like, I think that's activism. Activism is . . . oh man, I wish I could say things in a eloquent way. But I think you know taking action. But the kind that will, the kind that for me right now isn't expecting change but working for change. Because change is not just something that happens right away. All, all legendary activism it has been a movement, it has been something that takes a really long time and hurts a lot of people and . . . I don't know. I think it's just being part of that movement for change and taking action and trying to make that connection with people. It's really about people. Being, being part of a movement for change for people—not for the man or the system or like, you know, whatever that is. Because under that system there are people and they're like . . . I don't know, it's just like for, for the people I think.

Emerging from Alyssa's passionate response are several elements that support Felshin's (1995) definition of activism. Using words such as "practice," "working," "movement," and "connection" to describe her perspective, Alyssa is constructing a meaning for activism that demands large social involvement and a "change" to gauge activism's effectiveness. She also expresses the idea that what she counts as activism in the present moment is likely to shift with time and experience. Her hesitation to commit to a solid, singular definition demonstrates her understanding that one must "work for a change," that "change isn't something that happens right away," and that she herself may change. This point stands out sharply because it indicates that Alyssa understands that the results of her performance may not be able to be quantified. The artist who claims social responsibility may never gauge whether or not her words are effective precisely because performance is constantly under construction and the effects may not manifest while the artist is present. There are not always tangible effects of activist art. This can be frustrating, particularly due to Alyssa's repeated emphasis on seeking out a deep sense of connection with her broad audience through her performance. Similarly, Felshin (1995) suggests that an important attribute of activist art is "public participation . . . as a means of effecting social change," which implies a connection with the disenfranchised being made visible (9). The trouble is that there is no guarantee that participation by the public and/or connection with the artists' messages will be made. How can we even measure participation? If the public refuses to participate, does that subtract from the activist message? What if the message doesn't kick in until much later?

Alyssa continues shaping her definition of activism as "a movement . . . that takes a really long time and hurts lots of people. . . . it's really about people." Through her acknowledgment of people as the central focus of a broad understanding of activism, what Alyssa alludes to is a need for relationship building. One of her beginning statements sums it up best: "Theory to practice . . . that's activism." Alyssa points out an interesting division in how she defines activism and scholarship and clearly dictates that, to her, they are separate but related. What must occur is a deliberate development of scholarly work that is formulated on the premise of feasible transformation; small consistent practices that can be incorporated and supported without a large infrastructural system. This transformation must include intentional action taking with the purpose of shifting existing power relationships. This approach translates clearly when applied to the development of an artist, stretching the definition of scholarship to include activist performance, and, in turn, such performance is reflective of scholarship. As Carol Becker (2001) observes, "Few artist themselves are able to articulate the range of possible roles they might play, and even fewer were trained to see their function as parallel to that of the intellectual—and yet it is and should be" (110). I certainly didn't view my own artistic process and product as rigorous and activist and related to my pedagogy until the conclusion of the first year with Collective Energy and my first year of teaching on a collegiate level. I didn't have the language to do so, and I had internalized the belief that I was inferior to the sophisticated theory I was learning in my own graduate studies. I was also convinced that my work as an artist must be kept very separate from any scholarly work I attempted, because the two had no business mixing with one another.

It wasn't until after I read Patricia Hill Collins and Gloria Anzaldúa that I could see any part of my own reflection in my classrooms. Now I recognize how crucial the production of theory is as a form of activism, and yet this is only due to my exposure to the ways in which higher education can be made to suit the needs of my home community. This realization improved my personal connection to the art of teaching as well. I was not solely responsible for turning my privileged White students into champions for social change; all I had to do was expose them to the possibilities and dialogue with them. Critical pedagogy is about intentional partnership with my classroom students and about accountability for them and for me. We are all works in progress. My perspective of my own positions as teacher and artist began to shift and overlap, creating a new way for me to find agency in my classroom—ways that didn't rely on my embodiment or only on my personal experience as the avenue through which my students learned. Instead, they had to participate actively; they were accountable for cocreating the classroom community with me.

Meanwhile, Alyssa's particular history of international work centered on working within a community to provide people with critical, basic needs makes it easy to understand why her emphasis is on physical work and tangible outcomes instead of conversations or statements about social transformation. Her personal accounts of service also explain her hesitancy to identify herself as an activist. Alyssa points to a definition of activism that offers substance, or evidence, that action is being taken effectively, and she doesn't seem to recognize her own performance as a singer reflecting those qualities. From her perspective, the title of activism seems to only apply when the individual is directly and overtly involved in altering external social relations. However, it doesn't seem to acknowledge any "in-between" moments of activism: the moments that may occur during strategy planning sessions or rehearsals. The shifting that takes place along the spectrum of "theory to practice" doesn't seem to count for much to Alyssa.

What does carry importance is an ethic of hard work and commitment that is evident in Alyssa's admittance that, historically, activism "hurts lots of people." Performance is not always pretty or safe work to do, even when bathed by a spotlight. Alyssa recognized the possibility that she too might be hurt and perhaps had already experienced emotional distress because of her commitment to exploring activism through her performance. Privately, I always questioned if Alyssa was disappointed in her experience with Collective Energy because she didn't express fulfillment, nor did she seem quite sure of herself throughout the year. At a later point in our interview, she reveals the emotional costs of her personal commitment to performance and to activism. She describes her experiences through layers of relationships, her memories of performance, and her discussion of activism throughout her response that signals a correlation between these three areas of her life.

> Alyssa: I just like I'm so, so willing to be vulnerable sometimes and just willing to be affected and . . .
>
> Crystal: Yeah. That's what makes you effective . . . because it's absent in so many other people.

ALYSSA: It's really intense you know when you have that kind of like . . . or I guess what I feel like when I have that kind of like awareness that's always making me think, which puts me in a vulnerable situation, which other people really don't want to touch. Really intense.

CRYSTAL: It freaks them out.

ALYSSA: Yeah, it's intimidating I think . . . cuz I was thinking about it, would I want to? . . . it's so, for most people, satisfying to be simple, which I'm in no way putting down . . . but you know some people can accept that everything is the way it is and that's how it should be and that's how it's going to be and you know it's narrow and that makes me nervous. But I'm sure me being like that [spreads hands wide] makes other people nervous.

CRYSTAL: Right. Cuz they're not, they're not trained to look at it any other—

ALYSSA: They are satisfied.

CRYSTAL: Yeah.

ALYSSA: I'm not satisfied.

Feelings of restlessness and a commitment to remaining dissatisfied even at the cost of "making other people uncomfortable" and being misunderstood were undercurrents that moved throughout our conversation that day. Who the "other people" were remains a little vague for me. What is clear, however, is that Alyssa's desire to focus her own energies onto a singular strategy for achieving her activist goals seemed to be in opposition to her decision to remain open and "vulnerable." Activism for Alyssa was complicated because "for most people [it's] satisfying to be simple," yet, at the same time, her final sentence sums up her view of activism. Alyssa's version of activism meant that she was to remain unsatisfied until that slow process of change began to happen.

So, activism for Alyssa might also be a method for her to distinguish herself from fellow artists or her friends at university who choose to remain out of touch with issues she feels are urgent. Acknowledging her desire to become an activist is thus a means to recognize the traits that mark her difference from her peers. Claiming these traits and the desire for change makes her vulnerable and frustrated but also means that she deems vulnerability as valuable. If this is the case, then activism allows her to create her own community, defying boundaries drawn by ethnicity or class. Yet, identifying as an activist from this same standpoint would also require that Alyssa concede to the fact that *she* makes other people "uncomfortable," perhaps triggering a negative response from others due to her political performances and associations.

This discomfort is an embodied one, causing Alyssa to experience her distress on a visceral level because she is a White female who seeks out ways in which she can "be affected." For Alyssa, part of her search included becoming involved with Collective Energy. Her presence as the only self-identified White person in Collective Energy excludes her from participating with her White peers at university as they do, as if she engaged with the world by "accept[ing] the way everything is." On the other hand, her White body also performed for her within the group dynamics of Collective Energy and refused her a secure grasp on her position among the members. The shifting sands of discourse made it difficult for her to exercise a sense of ownership or authority in some of our performances and muted her during our group discussions. Although no one in Collective Energy ever vocalized a question of Alyssa's commitment to social change (in fact, they admired her), she described feelings of awkwardness and doubt in regard to her authority or ability to contribute to the group's performances and weekly discussions. This could be a result of many things—perhaps she was experiencing growing pains because of an increasing awareness of White privilege and the ways in which that privilege was at work even without her consciously taking advantage of it.

After hearing Alyssa's experience, I felt that this was a failure on my part as leader/teacher/mentor/friend for not knowing how to press out the prickly bubbles that reflected a misshapen being in her mirror so that she could see herself as I did: inspiring and dedicated. Alyssa's willingness to endure the discomfort of privilege and strategically employ the access afforded by that privilege to accomplish her objectives in the interest of social justice was in some ways the best action she could have taken. I also wondered if her performance counted as activist even if she didn't qualify herself as such. Alyssa continued to work toward crafting songs that expressed her passionate frustration as she searched for her place during our time in Collective Energy. She was attracted to the critical space for thinking opened up through our workshop meetings, and she was compelled to write and sing songs that communicated a similar critical view of her society—even at the expense of her membership in that society and even when that meant being critical of her work. At the same time, it was obvious that Alyssa felt like an outsider despite participating as a student artist in Collective Energy.

> Alyssa: . . . it never was so visible to me until Collective Energy I think when it was like that group of artists like so many different talents I was just like wow. Like I do have something to give and I think first coming into Collective Energy I was like, you know, what's my place here? I don't even know. I don't really know what I'm supposed to do or what is going to happen.

Alyssa's search for connection within Collective Energy as well as with her audience signifies several things to me: first, a pervasive feeling of inadequacy, as though her talent was not a worthwhile contribution, and second, an uncertainty that had a lot to do with race, although it was never explicitly stated as such. Not once during any of the transcripts I searched was I able to locate a conversation where I broached the subject of race in our weekly discussions. While ethnicity and culture were often the central themes in the performance pieces, somehow they never found their way into our reflexive conversations when Collective Energy met as a group, even while race was central to much of the artwork produced. Upon this discovery I reflected on the strangeness of that fact. Did I think that because we explored it through performance that the issues were adequately covered and clearly addressed? It's as if I assumed that because we all *appeared* different in our bodies and yet produced a cohesive performance that no further processing of how we operated through our difference within the group was necessary. Perhaps I refused the role of leader during these moments because I figured if it bothered them they would speak up about it. I didn't want to force things. I was also distracted by the work I was engaged in organizing and didn't pause to reflect on these things until the conclusion of the program. Yet I can clearly recall particularly relishing Alyssa's performances because they employed the element of surprise on the audience. The initial shock that registered on many of their faces once Alyssa began to sing gave me such pleasure. The reactions to Alyssa's voice ranged from confusion to delight that a stylish red-headed girl from a rural area could sing with such soulful conviction. Naming artists such as Nina Simone as one of her influences, Alyssa's performances in some ways appear to contradict and even betray the subjectivities that her White body might be inscribed with. As a budding feminist and double major in women's studies and journalism, Alyssa was well aware of what it meant to work through difference in a classroom setting. What became important to me was to convince Alyssa that her performance was a learning moment for her as an artist and the audience members as well, and because of that, her performance was activist.

Alyssa produced her specific version of history and experience, and that aggravated the social status quo that campus environments like Penn State perpetuate. Her choice to actively participate in a community of student artists that created performances designed to magnify their sense of social inequity was activist. Alyssa struggled to articulate the trouble she seemed to experience in the form of a desire to "feel a powerful connection" and her external responsibility to "be an artist so that what I do reflects who I am." Yet her wish remains unfulfilled because who she is always depends upon who others are not. I strove to make explicit for the student artists how those performances constitute a feminist sensibility that would continue to bear the consequences of such performance in, out, and around the classroom and community. Her musical performances were transformative because they refused an easy denial of the complex overlap of her privileges and her beliefs. Her choice to address and disrupt the privilege associated with her appearance as a White female through her performances that centralized such privilege was difficult emotional territory to navigate. I wasn't positive that I was equipped to guide her through it.

> Alyssa: I want to, I want to feel a connection. I, I'm going to be honest. I feel like an outsider . . . because I come from a rural area from . . . I grew up in . . . this is like in the middle of nowhere and like. . . . So but I, I feel like an outsider, but at the same time it feels very cool and I feel very . . . I feel welcomed, and I feel like this is a nice group, and I definitely want to get more into it and that because it's like I don't know. Something about having that urban setting in the middle of nowhere is like really cool, cause I've always been . . . And then it's . . . so I'm glad that we have that here. And but I need to . . . I can't pretend like I come from that setting, cause I don't. So I need to spend more time living it, spend more time in it you know like really feel that, and then I think I might really make the connection that I'm looking for. I think that will come later on.

However, Alyssa's journey for substance, for a practical strategy, and for a way to connect as an activist artist peaked during a particular moment. One night during a meeting, Alyssa shared a beautiful song entitled "Nothing But the Water," originally written and sung by Grace Potter and the

Nocturnals (2006). Although the lyrics weren't hers, Alyssa's delivery of the song was haunting and powerful. The song was so beautiful that Toby immediately jumped at the chance to collaborate with Alyssa on this particular piece. They scheduled time outside of our usual meetings to work on the piece. Because of Toby's additions to the piece, Alyssa seemed to discover deeper meaning in words she had sung many times before. Revising her performance assisted Alyssa by reinforcing the power she had even if she still viewed herself as a small drop in the bucket of a social change movement. Just as Collins (1999) lauded the daily refusal and resistance of Black women, through her partnership with Toby on this performance, Alyssa began to review and value more highly her own individual steps toward turning the status quo on its head, no matter how small those steps seemed. Both artists captured the audience because of the content of the piece; however their physical presence on the stage layered further meaning to an already potent performance. Alyssa was exploring herself as an artist extending beyond the typical ally position that so often those who enjoy White privilege limit themselves to.

The change in Alyssa's self-confidence and sense of belonging to Collective Energy shifted remarkably after she and Toby first performed this piece, even without the content or presentation being polished. Toby's desire to perform a duet with Alyssa yielded a sense of credibility to the performance because of the nature of Toby's role, not only in Collective Energy but as an instructor and director of the campus cultural center. This willingness to vouch for Alyssa undoubtedly gave her a confidence boost and immediately elevated the amount of visibility she had on campus as well. It was as if Alyssa's performance was a testimony to her self, and, although I didn't notice a perceptible shift in the way other members of Collective Energy interacted with her, Alyssa transmitted a new sense of ownership of her performances after the debut of "Water."

The initial revision of "Water" was performed during a meeting, then later introduced to a broader audience at our campus open mic, and finally was chosen as part of the repertoire that composed the culminating show Collective Energy presented at the University of West Indies in St. Augustine, Trinidad and Tobago. Audiences of no fewer than 250 students, staff, and faculty were in attendance at each performance of "Water" on campus. International and local travel exposed hundreds more to its message of reconciliation and revival of hope. Imagine what would happen if that performance were recorded, mass marketed, and made available for a larger audience. "Water" would then achieve another aspect of activist art because an even larger public would be invited to participate in the performance.

Each performance of "Water" offered a new rendering of what it means to be an activist, what it means for women to work together, and what it means to engage in the work of social relations across differences of race and privilege. Together, we bore witness to the power that lies in collaborative activist work.

Water

Original Song Lyrics by: Grace Potter (2006) "Nothing But the Water"
Adapted and performed by Alyssa
Original poetry by TJ Henry

Alyssa [sung]
I have seen what man can do
When the evil lives inside of you
Many are the weak the strong are few
But with the water, there is hope again

Toby
We got
Black is beautiful black power black liberation
Afros, cornrows, closed fists
We got
Macaroni and cheese, oxtail, collard greens
Low country cuisine
We got flashy cars and no sense of self
Designer clothes and no real wealth
We got
The latest dance, the hottest catch phrase
Like "holla," "that's gangsta," "respect the god"
We got a mother, sister, or uncle with no job
We got sex
America raping our minds
The satisfaction of a societal quickie then being left behind
Like a cheap ho
We had Martin, Malcolm, Garvey, Thurgood, and Mandela
We got young people that think life can't get no better
What we got is grabbing at straws and nothing to drink

Alyssa [sung]
Take me down to the levee

Toby
We've got to think and learn, work and yearn for nourishment
That can't fit through a straw

Alyssa [sung]
Take me down to the stream

Toby
We've got to push and shake, and bend and break
Social laws that leave us behind
That encourage us to confine our hopes and dreams into narrow
And dry streams

Alyssa [sung]
We're gonna wash our souls clean

Toby
Cause I'm trying to fill pails of opportunity for my people to drink

Alyssa [sung]
Take me down to the river
Take me down to the lake

Toby
Going down to the river, going in deep
Willing to sink trying to quench your thirst

Alyssa [sung]
Do it for the good Lord's sake

Toby [Alyssa hums behind Toby's words]
And I'll roll up these sleeves and I'll hike up this skirt
And I'll wade through waters of hard work to show you what you're worth
And I'll go in again, and again, giving and giving
And I'll come out of rough seas battered and cold
And damn near shivering
And I'll hold up that pail
And I'll tell you to
Drink self-confidence
Drink spiritual repentance

Drink these skills that I'll help you to build
Drink and be educated
And even when you're full, I'm going to pour the water on you
Because I can't stop until you're saturated
Until you drown in a future that runs as long and deep as the Nile
Until you're able to put boats on your river and be a guide to ghetto civilians
Until you're able to give a ride to one or a million
Until you're able to take my place and deliver
The hopes and dreams of living up the river
And even if you live in a city or suburb that makes it hard for you
to envision my words
Cause you don't see any oceans
There aren't any rivers around you
The wells of opportunity have run dry
Then we'll just have to try this in the kitchen sink
It's not a lot of water, but it's enough to drink
And we'll explore and seek opportunity anywhere we can
And we'll forget cups and pails
I'll catch it in my hand and I'll tell you to
Drink knowledge
Drink peace
Drink love
You've got permission to close your eyes and drink possibilities
that are fresh and new
Because you've got me
And I got you
I got you

Alyssa [sung forcefully]
Tried my hand at the Bible
Tried my hand at prayer
Oh, but nothing but the water is gonna bring my soul to rest
Oh, but nothing but the water
Is gonna bring my soul to rest

Toby and Alyssa began the piece seated in the center of the stage with their backs to one another, each facing either the left or right of the stage. Neither really looked at the audience. As the energy and momentum of the piece begins to crescendo, so did their emotion and volume. By Alyssa's line "Do it for the good Lord's sake" both performers were standing but still faced opposite directions. During Toby's final stanza, the two women slowly moved toward the center of the stage until they met facing one another. It becomes clear that they have been addressing one another throughout the piece, Alyssa calling for help and Toby assuring her that she is there to do just that.

Off the stage, the relationship Toby and Alyssa shared was that of mentor and mentee; Toby was well respected and held a position of authority, and Alyssa was one of her students and a frequent participant in many of the cultural programs Toby orchestrated. Their relationship is of particular significance because Toby is an African American woman and Alyssa is young and White. Their bodies contrast in appearance, but their performance was a complement of desire that charged this piece with a racial current that was not explicitly addressed in the words. Because of the racial dynamic, "Water" was instrumental in developing alternative discourses and opening new apertures for Alyssa to interact as a member of Collective Energy. On a larger scale, the unified front they presented on stage did not compromise either of their locations in regard to class, race, or background, and neither did it offer the audience an easy reading of their performance. Their artistic collaboration was centered on a mutual respect for the talent and commitment to one another, and also for their shared activist goals. bell hooks (2002) writes about how love and solidarity are necessary components of sisterhood. She states,

> Part of the process of becoming a feminist was to critique and change our sexist ways of seeing one another. Sisterhood wasn't just about what we shared in common—things like periods, obsessive concern with our looks, or bitching about men—it was about women learning how to care for one another and be in solidarity, not just when we have complaints or when we feel victimized. (130)

Although it would appear that Alyssa and Toby do not have much in common, since their life experiences have been vastly different simply based upon their physical appearances, their performance demonstrated determination to use their differences and positions in order to further their political activist goals. Because Alyssa sang the lines that communicated her weariness due to searching and seeking for a strategy to "bring her soul to rest," this marked her as a young woman in need of guidance. Toby, on the other hand, played the role of a woman who was leading the way, imparting her experience-based wisdom to a younger person. On an even deeper level,

Toby expressed her willingness to commit to the success of the young person by working hard to quench her thirst and then teach her how to find her own opportunities so that she could become self-sufficient. On the other hand, the performance of "Water" could be recast from an angle that forms a twisted shadow: consider the history in America of Black women sacrificing themselves on behalf of White women, inhabiting the roles of caretaker and "mammy" that serve to deny rather than attribute power to the woman of color. Performance, however, does not shy away from these contradictory readings. They are all accurate even as they compete, which is why performance is a useful method for exploring the convergence of relationship building, privilege, and power between Toby and Alyssa. While the historical context would appear at first glance to forfeit Toby's clout, her choice to school young Alyssa and the rest of her audience about her own life and successes is indicative of her subversive and overt occupation within that context. The environment of the debut of "Water" is important to note for yet another reading of Toby and Alyssa's performance. The audience at Bed consisted of a vast majority of students who looked up to Toby and consulted her for advice on a myriad of topics related to college and personal struggles. There was not a day that Toby's office on campus didn't have a steady stream of students visiting her, seeking guidance and connection with someone they firmly understood cared about them. On a larger scale, it was clear to the members of our campus community that Toby had indeed dedicated her life to creating opportunities for all of us to develop into self-sustainable leaders. We heard her poem and could testify to its truth. What I'm sharing here is the positive adjustments that I observed in Alyssa after the piece had been performed several times, which is the outcome that Toby's poem claims to desire. Although Toby, as an African American woman, is socially restricted, her liberation is revealed in the line where she gives permission to a young White woman to have confidence in herself and have peace of mind. Giving permission and allowing Alyssa access to the tools and fortitude to continue on her search for rest are Toby's strategies in this piece. She is positioning Alyssa to be accountable for her own actions and commitment to social change. Side by side they explore a landscape of discomfort together on a stage in a way that invited the other student artists and audiences to reconsider their own assumptions about race, gender, and power. It's also possible that this performance could be read as Alyssa simply singing background to Toby's poem, making Toby the prominent figure of focus. Such a reading would again recast the target(s) of Toby's poem, which might raise questions about the journey that she took in order to be a deliverer, a leader, a teacher. Who taught her how to be a leader? What are the values that drive her impassioned vision? Is Toby calling us to action as well?

If activism demands that attention be paid to the relationship that Alyssa was so intent upon building with her audience, and even more so with the other members of Collective Energy, then her performance of this piece with Toby showcased their activist strategy. Alyssa's earlier focus on practicality and action taking was outlined by Toby's words. It was interesting to note that the distractions Toby addressed in her opening lines particularly apply to young Black people, and yet Alyssa does not fit that description. Perhaps one of the lessons here is that Toby was sharing information that would be valuable for *any* young person, no matter how they culturally identified themselves. Understanding how broadly Toby's message can be applied is important because often in a university setting a person of color, especially a woman, does not hold a position of authority, and even if she does, it doesn't guarantee that her work or instruction is always valued by her White colleagues or students. In this case, however, I would venture to say that most students at our performances were well aware of Toby's position as director, and those who know her personally look up to her because she is such an exemplary role model. The point here is that Alyssa's search for direction signifies that Toby is equipped and qualified to lead White students, thus disrupting localized, traditional power structures that shape predominantly White institutions of higher learning. Toby's very performance breaks the "social laws" her poem refers to—she performs her activism, and her embodied enactment is representative of and resists, refuses, remixes broad ideologies and calls up the specificities of their immediate contexts simultaneously.

Toby's opening lines point out specific manifestations that appear to be symbols of success or arrival. She ends the first stanza by calling attention to the emptiness of "catch phrases" and "flashy cars" or "designer clothes" and suggests that people are lacking "sense of self." Alyssa's song introduces the piece with a sense of longing, acknowledging the terrible things she has witnessed "when the evil lives inside of you," yet she's asking for leadership and guidance. At this prompting, Toby calls for the hard work of "learning" and "yearning" that will aid in their efforts for satisfaction. But she makes it clear that opportunities don't simply appear, instead, "We've got to push and shake, and bend and break / Social laws that leave us behind." Toby again acknowledges that no one else is making an effort to remember or include "us" and that it will be a struggle to catch up with the rest of society. However, she continues to lay out her plan of action while Alyssa interrupts with lines asking to be brought to the water.

Alyssa's imploring words are met with Toby's urging to find water no matter the location that Alyssa may be in and to drink of the intangible yet very necessary offerings. Toby encourages her audience to drink qualities such as "peace," "love," "spiritual repentance," and "self-confidence." These characteristics are in stark contrast to the introduction of the poem where material goods defined success. However, she continues to list "education," "skills," and "knowledge," which once developed can *lead* to material success and the ability to be self-sufficient. Toby demands that the quality of the listener's life be improved on both a spiritual/mental/emotional level and on a visceral/physical/financial level as well. She does not neglect the practical necessities of life, and neither does she ignore the needs of the soul. Toby's reasoning behind naming these specific qualities is to develop autonomy and self-efficacy so that the listener will be capable of replacing Toby by "taking my place [to] deliver the hopes and dreams of living up the river." Toby acknowledges her role as a mentor and embraces the label of teacher. Because Toby performs these lines directly to Alyssa on the stage, she is committing herself to guiding and training Alyssa and the students Alyssa represents until the day Alyssa will be saturated "in a future that runs as long and deep as the Nile," leading others to the water when Toby is no longer able to, ensuring that the next generation will have access to "drink possibilities that are fresh and new."

Alyssa closes the piece with a strong finish, listing the various other methods she has tried to find "rest" for her soul. It is not until she receives Toby's help that she is able to draw the conclusion that "nothing but the water" will give her peace. Toby's assurance that "you got me and I got you" works to reinforce the collaborative relationship that is necessary for achieving their goal of enabling others to "explore and seek opportunity anywhere we can" so that "knowledge," "peace," and "love" are being consumed and shared. The choreography of their performance on the stage further emphasized how powerful it can be and how necessary it is to be taught and trained and to be receptive of the guidance offered by those who demonstrate support through their work with another person. This type of relationship requires an experienced mentor willing to share what she knows, be generous with what she has, and be humble enough to allow someone else to take the lead. It also demands a student willing to learn, to be disciplined in order to become masterful, and to surrender her gifts and energy for a purpose she may not fully comprehend. It seems to me that this is often the case when one must learn something new. This relationship, this poem, this entire project was about sacrifice. And through this performance, activism became something relatable, attainable, and practical.

Activism was performed in a relevant way, provoking questions about who is qualified to lead and what it means to be responsible through interracial social relations and addressing desires for financial stability, well-being, and emotional fulfillment while suggesting a strategy for achieving them.

Another important aspect of "Water" was the explicit connection made between activism and political action. What makes this connection extraordinary was the direct correlation between self, family, and politics. Basically, Toby suggested that helping one's family and helping oneself are political actions. Drawing on the feminist slogan that the personal is political, Toby and Alyssa have performed a version of feminism that places the family and a holistic sense of self-sufficiency at the forefront of conversation. Part of what makes "Water" so compelling is that it pulls on difficult individual and familial experiences and makes those experiences available to an audience while presenting the social and political forces that have contributed to the negative effects caused by those experiences. Because Toby and Alyssa not only addressed those experiences but constructed and committed to a plan to actively alter the state of being "thirsty," the difficult situations are brought to light, and awareness of the factors causing those conditions is made apparent to the audience. In this way, "Water" is intentionally designed as a political performance of oppression as well as a plan for transformation, subverting the negative through solidarity.

Peggy Phelan (1993) writes of the benefit and downfall of performance art by saying that its resistance to mass reproduction is its greatest political strength (149). While it is easy to understand Phelan's connection between the political potency of performance art and her reasoning that a "mass reproduction" of such work would water down the political effectiveness of an organic experience, this assumption raises several issues. If a goal of feminist activist art is to expose and involve the public at large, then what are the consequences of resisting large numbers of duplication of these performances? In fact, I question if performance can be reproduced at all. If it is based upon the premise that each performance is a new rendering and a reconstruction whose content depends upon the actual moment that performance takes place and the audience that is present, then can performance be reproduced at all? In addition, the particular audience that has access to performance art constitutes a significant portion of its political nature. There is an all too familiar gleam of exclusivity that lies beneath the surface of valuing that only a handful of folks may be invited to participate in the potentially powerful and specific politicalness that performance art can offer up. This restriction on who will have access to performing as an artist and, more to my point here, participating as an audience member, calls up images of our educational and governmental systems rooted in a tradition of elitist principals and unjust gatekeepers.

I would argue that an artist invested in social change would be inclined to subscribe to the contrary: accessibility by the community/audience/masses is of the utmost importance. A large chunk of my motivation for teaching and raising awareness is to grow the level of criticism to match the level of consumption of popular culture and the media in our students. The example that comes to my mind immediately is the political movement that birthed the music of hip hop. However, this is not due to mass reproduction as Phelan suggests; it is due to a lack of critical cultural understanding, production, and consumption on the part of the artist and on the part of the community as well as capitalist interests of the recording industry (Bynoe 2004). Another aspect of the political disconnect circles back to the previous section on the student artists' struggle to explore social responsibility. Values are emerging that conflict with the roots of the music and art form that we practice. Besides that, oppressed groups value different things and social issues are not prioritized uniformly across the board. Also begging to be considered is the evolution of what it means for students today to be politically strong. I offer that honing the skill and craft of creating and performing potent spoken word as a method of cultural development, social criticism, and expression is a viable practice. Negotiating cultural development through performances allows the public a strategy and an educational opportunity to try to recreate for themselves the source of authority and sense of autonomy that performance art appears to provide. I find it more politically useful to expose and educate many on the method and technique and ask them to try it and to think about it rather than to maintain its elite and exclusive VIP status.

Carol Becker (1994) continues to comment on the effectiveness of art as a form of activism and why it is important that art fulfill its role by presenting reality as a problem. She goes on to state that art becomes "problematic precisely because reality has become non-problematic. The more that is hidden and suppressed, the more simplistic the representation of daily life, the more one-dimensional and caught in the dominant ideology the society is, the more art must reveal" (xiii). Becker's quote links back to Alyssa's definition of activism and her frustration that "other people" (perhaps in this case, non-artists or nonperformers) were satisfied to remain "simple." What Becker is asking of activist art is that it acts as an exposure. Activist art cannot be afraid of the dark or what is in plain view but denied. Activist art must make the invisible seen and *felt*. There is no disguise left, no smoothness. This level of vulnerability is quite terrifying—imagining the world with no makeup, no costume. Activist art demands that the artist digests reality and that the audience watches and participates. Cherríe Moraga (1981) explains the motivation that fuels the efforts that go into presenting reality as one-dimensional: fear. She says,

> . . . for each of us has in some way been both oppressed and the oppressor. We are afraid to look at how we have failed each other. We are afraid to see how we have taken the values of our oppressor into our hearts and turned them against our selves and one another. (32)

According to Becker (1994), providing and demanding a vision of reality is one of the most important functions of art with an activist intention. The student artists who participated by composing and performing their original poetry exposed their participation as both oppressor and oppressed and the way such participation impacted their reality for an audience made up of both strangers and friends. Working to make visible and perform the contradiction of values that we occupy is risky business for the student artists and for the audience. However dangerous it may be, this risk is necessary. Performing the contradiction is the only way to uncover and explore the ways we are connected. Moraga's (1981) quote points out how essential visibility is for recognizing the ways in which multiple subjectivities can be performed at one time from the same source even when they contradict. Performance poetry served Collective Energy as a way to embody and play out the consequences of employing the "values of the oppressor." The composition of spoken word and song provides an avenue for recognizing how we have hurt ourselves and one another, a way to read the multiple discourses of the self, and also provides access to imagine another way to exist by honing in on the overlaps. What a heavy load of responsibility. As Alyssa admitted earlier, activism as she recognized it "hurts a lot of people," and perhaps her hesitancy in labeling her art as activist is related to her desire to protect others as well as herself. Maybe she wanted to refuse the label of activist and thus refuse to expose and potentially embarrass anyone as a result of her performance. Perhaps this is a gendered issue as well.

In my earlier mention of Carlos's work with "Shooter" and his employment of violent metaphors to position himself as socially responsible, he didn't seem to have a problem with the fact that he or his audience may be wounded. He even spoke of his expectation that his spoken word poetry would unleash his own demons, marring himself in the process. Alyssa, on the other hand, seems to seek healing through her performance and is dedicated to the idea of connections and relationships that are holistic and full of forgiveness and reflection. How was I to design an experience to take into account both of these desires? What sort of space had enough room for the discursive conditions that were being participated in by both Carlos and Alyssa? How would they be equipped to transcend and alter their realities and gendered construction? Was the stage and space we set large and liberated enough to meet the criteria for both of these perspectives? I learned that performance is elastic and can be stretched around awkward positions. Collective Energy accommodated both perspectives because each of them was performed at some point throughout the experience; the contradiction, the friction, was performed without necessarily being identified, labeled, and reviewed in our discussions at the precise moment they were performed.

I have also learned that the junctures of activism and art demand flexibility. I discovered that my own existing ideas of activist art and the ways activism can be employed and taught were troubled from the outset because I did not account for difference—in the performances or in the workshops—nor could I have predicted the parts of the performances or the workshops that might be met with resistance from the audience or student artists. There is no way to control the outcome, and that is not easy for me to deal with. However, this disturbance is productive because it serves now to highlight the gaps and omissions in the original design of the Collective Energy experience. Reflecting on the way the experience was constructed is also helpful because I realize that no matter the changes that might be made in the curriculum, the members who participate in Collective Energy will always determine the outcome. So while I can expand and narrow the focus, it is the student artists and their audiences who will ultimately decide what the tone and content of the program will be.

Although the standpoints and performances of Carlos and Alyssa are marked by the labels of male and female, Black and White, perhaps they cannot be mapped as contradictions. Both are in pursuit of responsibility and community uplift. Both seek to create a bridge between their experience and that of the audience. Each also reflects the other: sometimes violent, constantly implicating the self. Both value and respect a sense of justice and equity, although they reconfigure these ideologies for the audience as well. Both are denied access by the world because of the values and experiences that drive their performances.

"Art refuses to be easy," reminds Becker (2004, xiii). Activist art is full of refusal: refusal of labels, refusal of boundaries, and refusal of the reproduction of status quo performances. However, I'm not certain that I communicated to the student artists why naming our performance "activist" had significance. While I clearly understood that discourses operate as constantly in competition and that those discourses shift within different communities, the student artists hesitated to agree or even engage in this discussion. Instead of refusing the label of "activist art" for what we produced, I worked to challenge them to interrogate their own performances and how they might be received by the audience. Performance functioned as a conveyor vehicle, full to the brim with meaning and emotion, that traveled from the camp of student artists to somewhere in the middle of their mainstream and majority. The student artists occasionally voiced a desire to catch a ride with performance to travel to the center of the mainstream as well, so that performance became the strategy of their activism, parking and depositing them and their messages from the outskirts to center stage. However, at the end of the experience, because several of the student artists, including Alyssa, were uncomfortable naming themselves or their art "activist," I had to reconsider what the language meant to this generation. We often used the terms "social responsibility" or "social justice" instead of activist, but it seemed as if several of the student artists were uncomfortable with any label whatsoever.

> JONATHAN: I don't really have anything social justice—
>
> TOBY: Everything is social justice—
>
> Q: It's what's in your heart.
>
> JONATHAN: I'm trying to find like, my niche—

Here Jonathan gives an example of the rootedness that seemed ever present in our discussions. The hesitancy he expressed could be a result of the pressure he felt to commit to a label or category he wasn't sure he fit. I understand this cautionary approach because labels imply limits. The idea that being activist would prevent Jonathan from producing art on any topic he was inspired to create around is one that seemed to be engrained in the minds of the student artists. Drawing this boundary seemed to indicate a lack of understanding about the ability to occupy several discourses and subjectivities at once.

I am mixed, a mixture, in all aspects of my intersectional life; I couldn't even choose just one doctoral program—even my Ph D is a dual degree. My mixture is explicit in my body and in the intentional choices that I make.

I have come to understand that being multiple things in an undeniable, embodied way has dictated the way I move through the world, and I have learned how to find power in that. So, it's no surprise that I helped to design Collective Energy with a mixture of everything: ethnicities, socioeconomic statuses, and talents, in order to create a space where we were all forced into the awareness that we each inhabited multiple identities simultaneously. Our residence and active participation in these multiple places ought to be expressed through our art. When we expressed them, we demonstrated the ways that we were connected, the ways we lived together and performed together with others, and would eventually show how our performances of personal experiences, when contextualized against and in between one another, were indeed activist. What appeared to remain unclear for some of the student artists was the way their performances counted as the transition of theory to practice that Alyssa cited in her definition of activism. We spoke frequently of the relationships between people that were affected and cultivated, but we did not focus on the relationship that existed between words and actions. Performance is both of these things at once, the ultimate culmination of theory meets practice. Toby and Tony elaborate:

> TONY: You have to be responsible to some degree for what comes out of your mouth. Not saying don't use bad words or whatever, but for the message, how that comes out . . . although you can't control how people—
>
> TOBY: Words can motivate action. Being mindful what type of action could occur as a result. Because a lot of people in the past have gotten off on, you know, "I'm not a role model" . . . but you still have a responsibility for whatever the hell you write and what you put out there. So owning that responsibility and recognizing that in some ways, you are responsible for what's in the world when you spit, rap, or whatever.

When Toby states that the performer is directly "responsible for what's in the world," she suggests that performance is a way of recreating the world. Adjustments or alterations might be made as a result of a performance, and this is a responsibility to be recognized. Tony agreed that "the message" of the artist always exists and is transferred whether she chooses to acknowledge it or not. This idea stands in direct opposition to two things: first, the overabundance of celebrities in hip hop and popular culture who vehemently deny any allegations that they are a role model for their listeners and supporters (Kitwana 2002). Lawsuits and efforts to censor music and other types of media demonstrate that there is at the very least a correlation between cultural intake and the formation of ideology and behavior. The larger question is to what degree is the artist or the audience held responsible for what might ensue as a result of a performance? This line of thought returns us to the messy conversation about the socially responsible artist. How does material success factor into the career of an activist artist?

Second, and most closely related to Collective Energy's experience, is the issue that the student artists did not immediately view themselves as viable cultural producers. Asking them to rethink their performance in terms of implementing social change and through an activist lens was a long leap. At some point during their lives, each member had been pointedly told that their views, experiences, and versions of history (and therefore of the future) were illegitimate. How could I expect them to take their work seriously?

Visual artist Elizam Escobar (1994) posits that most "cultural activity is mainly seen as entertainment and is not supposed to be a critical activity—an activity that allows you to think critically about lived relations to the world and especially about immediate relations to society" (51). Escobar's reference to critical thinking again points in the direction of space that Collective Energy provided through the weekly workshop meetings. These meetings and rehearsal spaces were opportunities for the student artists to rehearse the creation, development, and critical reflection of art focused on their issues. I wanted these students to know that our weekly workshops were constructed to respond to their concerns about not being taken seriously, and to address the difficulty they have viewing themselves as legitimate cultural producers. Their trouble is no surprise, since most of their peers have been trained by the influx of popular culture to expect to be kept entertained and distracted instead of provoked to think and to consider how they might be implicated in the society in which they live. When the performances that Collective Energy produced are critical of the lived relations we share, they are using art to question a reality presented to them through the media and the history textbooks of their classrooms. This is art that calls up the relations we are situated in with one another and with society at large, and it interrogates the role that we each play in those relationships.

The student artists may not have all shared in my politically focused goals for our performances. They also might never be permanently labeled as activist because of the shifty nature of slipping positions and blurred boundaries that mark territories. Activism is a process—just as performance is—something to work through and toward and within. To be seen and heard, to be witnessed and accounted for, seemed to gratify the student artists' immediate wish for social transformation. The social context required by activist art granted them the public space to contextualize their internal experiences in order to develop external or visible concepts of social transformation. Participating in discourses that positioned them as activists is possible only to the extent that they recognize themselves and are recognized by their audience as such. Their level of resistance and desire to pursue a resistant stance was driven in different ways dependent upon their position once their invisible survival techniques and their sense of politics were exposed. Although not directly addressing performance, Bronwyn Davies offers a look into the possibilities that can be applied to performance.

> By making visible the ways in which power shifts dramatically, depending on how subjects are positioned by and within the multiple and competing discourses they encounter, they can begin to imagine how to reposition themselves, realign themselves, and use the power of discourse they have to disrupt those of its effects they wish to resist. (Davies 2000, 180)

Performance is an invitation to audition those repositionings and realignments over and over again. Performance provides a space to stage the disruptions of power on a large and small scale. Performance calls attention to the contradiction of the discursive practices of the audience member while acknowledging how the performer self-interprets and self-identifies. Meanwhile, the audience members actively sift and construct the performer, organizing the performance in a way that makes sense to them and according to the discourses they find themselves positioned in and that they construct collectively as audience members. The performer also calls attention to the collective discourse in which they are all participating. In this way, performance is an invitation to be something besides what you usually see yourself as. It is a chance to do something different. Davies (2000) continues, "Language is understood as the most powerful constitutive force shaping what we understand as possible and what we desire within those possibilities" (181). Through understanding their own fluid position as subjects of many different discourses, the performers and audience have the agency to imagine themselves differently.

Imagination is indeed required for the practice of spoken word poetry performance. If we are interested in resisting the ways we are told to live and behave, then we must create alternatives. If we have grown tired of the dominant discourses that pervade and legitimize or discredit our histories and our futures, then we must begin to imagine how things can be different for us. In order to imagine new ideas, we have to begin to think differently about how we treat ourselves and each other. If we cannot exercise an ethic of care and respect in our most intimate of spaces—our minds and spirits and hearts—about our own well-being, then how can we expect to shift any larger structural institutionalized framework? We must imagine a new way to perform love. There must be a change in the way we perceive our ability to interact with one another if we want to also imagine a new way to resist the old system that enforces inequality and abuse of power. There arose an interesting overlap of the subject of activism or resistance and the subject of love and what that meant to the socially responsible artist during Collective Energy's experience.

4

Acts of Love

Love can help me know my name.

—Seal, "Love's Divine"

Like a moth to a flame I find myself drawn to work that denies me any sound closure. Even the dramatic structure of a play includes an introduction, a climb in intensity, a peak, and then plateau. Looking back I wonder where we were supposed to climax, and I check myself for signs of satisfaction: I find few, if any. No layer of my life provides tidy endings. Teaching is a tease, performing is an addictive drug, and my relationships? Well, they tend to be circular. How do we let go? Why do we hold on? At what point do I give the final push to extricate this large project out of my self? Is that even a possibility or a desire? Or am I simply trying to do as I've been trained to do. Do I just want to pass? And you, dear reader. Can you measure what you have just witnessed across these pages? Or, like the magician, have I run out of tricks up my sleeve with which to distract you? The trail we have hiked has been varied in terrain, the weather has been unkind, and I worry that I have not properly guided you. At this rate, you will never find your way back. Neither will I. This has been a scrapbook of memories that fade in comparison to the vivid experience I have shared with a group of people, but it is all I have to offer you here. This is a forensic collection of clues to a case that remains unsolved.

By performing the very structures that separate and confine us, Collective Energy has been a menace to our restrictive limits. Although wide in variety, it has been the contradictions, competing discourses, and difficult choices that the writing and performances of our group have used as the stuff for the stage. Whether it is the intersection of social responsibility with accessibility and exposure or the ideal of activism and how that meets resistance and real life, these crossroads are where decisions are made. They are the locations of in-between, of mixture, where actors choose the roles they will play. This has not been a handbook that will end with clear outlines for best practices or mathematical equations that are certain in their sums. Instead, this is a valley of decision where perspective determines discourse and action. The intersection I leave you in is crowded with lonely artists looking for connection and hustling poets trying to make a living. This is the navy blue sky of dusk. Not quite bright enough to be considered daytime, but not dark as night either. This is the moment at the end of the day when I ask, Have I done all I can do? This is the moment when you ask, Where do I turn from here?

I have worked thus far in an effort to critique and question an experience that I played a leadership role in and participated in fully as a member. I have been blown away by my time with Collective Energy and have focused on our first year together as a means to learn about the ways that performance and pedagogy go hand in hand with resistance, recognizing our selves as subjects and artists and researchers, and how these moments of intense connection and disconnection have affected our social relationships. I have worked to locate my presence within this work, and although it has not been a painless experience, it is one that I hope contributed in some way to Collective Energy's betterment—that it in some way complemented and complicated their lives. The fact is, I feel an overwhelming sense of love for each of these students individually and an appreciation for the process we went through. And so, working at my best to maintain integrity and to be true to the passionate swelling of love that I feel, I focus upon a brief discussion of love and ethics and the ways my own performance has served me in teaching and especially learning about the practice of both. I posit that although the relationship between love and ethics is not always recognized, both elements are always present in the discourse about one or the other. The necessarily cooperative existence of love and ethics provide an interesting and, for me, a useful opening through which I can translate the experiences I have had as a leader and performer with Collective Energy. I suggest that it might also be helpful to make love and ethics the grounding and central motivation behind other theoretical and activist work that takes place within and beyond the academy. Ethics determine and construct concepts about love, and love is conceptualized and enacted because of how ethics are put into practice.

What's Love Got to Do with It?

In her body of work aptly titled *All About Love*, cultural critic bell hooks describes love as characterized by possessing qualities of "care, affection, recognition, respect, commitment and trust, as well as honest and open communication" (2000, 3). She insists that a feeling of connection is not the same as love; instead love is a willful choice we make. If we have to make a choice to love, then that implies two things: first, to love is to accept responsibility. Second, love is not an instinct we inherently have—it is a verb. Love is an action word. According to hooks, "to begin thinking of love as an action rather than a feeling . . . automatically assumes accountability and responsibility" (2000, 13). This assumption of accountability to others and responsibility for the effects that result from choices we make is an intersection where love and ethics begin to relate to one another. For the duration of our time together, the student artists and I continued to struggle with the notion of social responsibility and how overlaying even our love poems with that sense of duty removed the illusion of neutrality.

Consequences, whether positive or negative, result from actions, and this contradicts much of what we are socialized to believe about love. Talk of a conscious practice of self-discipline, which is sometimes unpleasant to think about, seems to have no place in dialogue with the socialized norms the media perpetuates in regard to romantic relationships. Thinking of love as a duty that requires commitment even when it's no longer fun or romantic is not enticing, especially when "popular culture messages declare the meaningless of love, its irrelevance," through movies and fairy tale–type endings (hooks 2000, xviii). However, love in its purest form is discipline. Any lifestyle change demands self-discipline and purposeful habit formation, such as a careful diet and regular exercise for a healthy body, so why should love be different? It is not always easy or natural. Think about our classrooms, our work relationships—the majority of the spaces in which most of our time is spent does not allow for the reflective conversations needed to work through new notions of love. Collective Energy's weekly meetings, however, did just that. The meetings opened up a new space for figuring out what it was we were feeling and thinking. More importantly, we had a chance to discuss why and how we arrived at those beliefs. Because we were so intentional in our focus on the qualities of a socially responsible artist or performance, our discussions were already foregrounded in social, racial, and gender issues, making the most intimate and personal (and deceptively private) political once again.

We discussed the ways to qualify what counted as socially responsible artistry. There seemed to be a division between what the group counted as political poems and what they considered love poems. I found this tremendously interesting and disturbing at the same time. Uncertainty pervaded the following conversation, and I couldn't help but notice that Toby and I argued adamantly to persuade them otherwise.

> TONY: I think mine is a mix of all things. I do write love poems a lot, but I think of that, to some degree, that's socially responsible, maybe?
>
> CARLOS: Well, that's—
>
> TONY: That's a strong emotion that helps uplift people in oppressed groups . . . but at the same time—
>
> CRYSTAL: At the same time when we say we want to represent the fullness of a cultural experience of a people, love is a cultural experience.
>
> TOBY: And I talk about, like how bell hooks talks about how no one brings up "love ethic" anymore, um, and how important that is. Like you said uplifting people or whatever but even just creating a positive vibe, um, in a community, um talking about love and showing love and how important that is. So love is an act of social responsibility.
>
> JONATHAN: I don't really have anything "social justice"—
>
> TOBY: Everything is social justice—
>
> Q: It's what's in your heart.
>
> JONATHAN: I'm trying to find like, my niche—
>
> TONY: Talking about love is social responsibility, and it's you—I hear *you* . . .
>
> STACEY: It's something beyond your brain or your heart. It's like that tiny, deep, deep part of your soul. The deepest emotion . . . it touches places in me . . . it's supernatural . . .

> TOBY: It's not trite; it challenges people to understand what Love is. Challenging people to look at things they thought they knew. That's love ethic. And really, that's what love is all about.

It is still unclear whether or not the other members of Collective Energy fully grasped and agreed that a love ethic was the driving force that shaped their experience; however, one thing they did learn that night was that it shaped the way Toby and I approached leadership. I suspect the hesitation from Jonathan, Carlos, and initially Tony to acknowledge love as political territory was in part an effort to avoid marking themselves as overtly political artists. Perhaps it was fearsome territory for these considerably new performers to immediately commit to a label.

The careful evasion of being labeled as political or feminist can be looked at in several ways. First, perhaps the males were making an effort at preventing any label at all, drawing an interesting and very apparent gendered line. Carlos, for example, said one of the things he loved best about performing was "freedom to express myself." Most of the student artists expressed their relief at the liberation they found in performing without the perceived hindrance of expectations. While these ideas point to a romantic view of the performance space—desiring carefree performances that outsmart the audience in order to avoid being named into a category or shoved into a "box"—there was some truth to the theory that performance was liberating. I don't agree that there is any escape from the interpretation of the audience, but I do believe the stage offers a moment to face those interpretations, inaccurate though they may be. Such boldness has escaped me personally in other contexts, and so it is not hard to understand why the student artists may shy away from consciously adding more conflict to the site of the stage where they have felt strong and certain.

Another idea is that perhaps the boys felt as if it was dangerous territory to claim to be political. Prior to any performance that took place during our time together, there was already considerable pressure and nervousness about how well they would be received; also, for Jonathan and Tony in particular, they were comfortable writing and performing around tender themes of romantic love. They were accustomed to a certain positive reception by the audience after these performances. Actually auditioning a new performance persona or attempting to purposefully write on a "political" topic was a difficult test. What if the crowd didn't like their new attempts? What if no one clapped for them? Although these fears went unspoken during our conversation that Tuesday night, I had a sneaking suspicion that the boys were somehow trying to ensure that they would not let down their peers or themselves. The final concern that may have been woven through their refusal of addressing love as a political issue was their location as they are situated in a broader conversation. As young male artists of color, Jonathan, Tony, and Carlos are presented with limited options that would mark "appropriate" participation in conversations, behaviors, and responses to both love and politics. They were more familiar with how to address and present socially acceptable versions of love. Besides, politics was for militant brothers who wanted to overthrow the government, right?

Although this misconception morphed over the year as we worked and studied and rehearsed together, the young men of Collective Energy were always acutely aware that it was hazardous for them to be overtly political. I showed them examples of other spoken word artists of high reputation (such as Will "Da Real One" Bell, Dwayne Morgan, Marco Mercado, Nathan James, Hamza the Seventh Son, Heru Ofori-Atta, and Amir Sulaiman), who are well known and highly respected by diverse audiences for their unapologetically explicit portrayal of politics in their work. However, even most of the examples I shared with them had suffered some severe form of legal regulation such as FBI investigation, police brutality, or rejection and acidic criticism from predominantly white mainstream popular culture. Given such consequences, it is a small wonder that Jonathan, Tony, and Carlos, with their high hopes and vivid dreams of material success and equally lucid determination to groom themselves as writers and performers, hesitated at making a blatantly political choice in their artwork early on.

Within this moment of conversation, however, it is interesting to note that Tony moves from noting the "mixed" content in his poetry and his timid question that "maybe" writing about love was an act of social responsibility to his certain declaration of it. Tony decidedly claims his territory as both a love poet and a socially responsible artist. Even more interesting is Tony's insistence that he authentically recognizes Jonathan within his love songs by saying "it's you—I hear *you*" and therefore identifies Jonathan clearly as a socially responsible artist without Jonathan's acquiescence. This is an example of a moment when a subject is located within a discourse he did not choose for himself. Jonathan was assigned membership as a socially responsible artist, despite the fact that he had no desire to be any such thing.

In another light, this moment represents an interesting convolution of the women's standpoint on the notion of love and politics. None of the female members of Collective Energy articulated an issue or disagreement with the suggestion that writing or performing pieces focused on love were anything other than a socially responsible act. Q felt so passionately about it that she interrupts Toby while trying to convince Jonathan that "it's what's in your heart." For Q, there was no separation of matters of the heart and matters of the state. This is a positive and encouraging statement because it means that Q understands her own feelings and experiences as valid and worthwhile, and she also communicates that sharing them with others through her spoken word works to legitimize her views on these matters.

At the same time, Stacey, who earlier spoke out about not feeling an emotional attachment to her poetry eloquently states that love is a feeling "beyond your brain or your heart," meaning that it is not something that is always intellectually stimulated or emotionally supported, and she hints that love has the ability to "touch" that "deep, deep part of your soul" because it is "supernatural." Her statement infers that love is spiritual and therefore more sacred and prevailing than either the brain or the heart. And although experiences or conversations of love have become trivialized because they appear to be the subject or at least side plot in most heteronormative media, Toby concludes that "it's not trite," reiterating that everyone's contributions to the conversation that night were of value.

These young women artists often spoke of love within their work and performed love as a powerful force that should be taken seriously. Sometimes their performance of love was sexual in nature, as in Stacey's piece that included a line advising her mate to "get out the handcuffs and the mirror / we're gonna be grown tonight." Sometimes love showed up through the proclamation of a desire to "bring the humility back to love / where it's no longer about him or me / but what we can be . . . together" as in Toby's piece entitled "Ride or Die." At the same time, and often throughout the same poem, these young women also displayed no hesitancy when candidly making references that left little question about their expressly uncensored political beliefs. Q's debut performance at an open mic consisted of a piece entitled "Love and War," which used the metaphor of a troubled love relationship and compared that turmoil with the current state of the US government.

These young women did not share in the hesitation of their male counterparts about claiming their right and desire to talk about many representations of love, and when the same sense of momentary freedom that Carlos pointed out earlier was made available to them through the medium of performance, they reveled in it. Although they did not verbalize the ways they may have paid personally for that moment of brave artistic release, I'm almost certain they struggled with being forcibly categorized by the audience as well. The subject positions made available to them by the audience or through their daily lives did not account for the overlap and integration of their lived and performed experiences. Sexual or spiritual, romantic or revolutionary—the familiar Madonna/whore or militant/sellout dichotomies continued to restrain and oppress the student artists no matter their gender. Serious queries faced us. What if their poems were too sexual and they were ostracized or mistreated by their peers? What if they were in an intimate relationship and their partner felt that intimate privacy had been jeopardized? What if they were no longer taken seriously as socially responsible artists because they choose to include songs and stories of love in their work? While the women's obstacles did not lie in a fear of addressing either love *or* politics, they still faced stakes for considering the relationship *between* the two subjects. Any time a female artist gambles by dancing on the borders of the in-between of her subjectivity and experiences, she runs the risk of being pushed to either side by a public uncomfortable with traipsing through that ambiguous territory along with her. Early on, the girls were in danger of being too political and thus deemed extremists or—heaven forbid—feminists by a crowd who may not appreciate their socially responsible stance and may prefer to have their love and their politics sold separately.

Because of Toby's experience and willingness to share her insight, within the layers of this discussion lay the concept of "challenging people" used in a positive light—being critical of relationships, of perspectives and views, of what is named love and the ways that we are recognized. Performing out of an understanding that the artist is a pedagogue and that performance can be motivated by a love ethic requires confrontation with other more common discourses that state the opposite. Performing out of an ethic of love means being willing to fight through those discourses and their consequences, challenge them, and at the same time challenge the more powerful who hold and perpetrate those ideologies. Indeed, Carol Becker (2001) states, "The best art goes so far into the personal that it actually broadens its own particularity and touches the world" (109). For the student artist, risking such a deep connection by sharing a love song or poem in a public open mic hosted on the same campus where they live is a decidedly political move; it is an effort to touch that "deep, deep place" in someone other than the self, moving focus back and forth between the individual and the outside institutions that are always shaping us. These student artists weren't just performers—they had to face the audience members who knew them offstage as well. Any social norms the student artists critiqued, any misinterpretation or intimate detail they shared, would have to be accounted for in an immediate way. Their artistic adventures were not detached from their lives on campus—there were faculty in attendance at the open mics as well. How might these students face consequences within a classroom setting by their professors? How might their words be used against them?

To challenge beliefs that parrot dominant narratives and most especially when those narratives reinforce social expectations about love is to ask for conflict. This site of confrontation is, however, a rich teaching and learning opportunity. If we can understand the investments and rewards that accompany upholding mainstream beliefs about love, then we can better dismantle them or build upon them. If student artists have a space to imagine loving and love in a way that positions them as powerful or at least equal, then the dynamics of their relationships might improve. The concept of working at love requires that we recondition our expectations of what it means to love and the ways in which love is demonstrated through performance.

A Performance of Love

Defining love gets even more complicated, and hooks (2000) continues to provide an explanation as to why that may be. She claims that the coexistence of love and abuse is impossible, which is the reason why in the midst of participating in dysfunctional relationships "it is so difficult for most of us to embrace a definition of love that would no longer enable us to see love as present in our families" (4). Investing in the definition of hooks's love requires honesty so severe that it may be painful. What if our families never taught us how to love because *they* didn't know how? As a result, love also requires that the capability to forgive be developed. If love is something we learn how to do, does that mean we can relearn it as well? Nel Noddings (1984) disagrees. In her theory that discusses "an ethic of caring" as a classroom practice for instructors, she suggests that while "one who is concerned with behaving ethically strives always to preserve or convert a given relation into a caring relation," she insists that "acting out of caring, one calls on a sense of duty or special obligation only when love or inclination fails" (173–174). In other words, Noddings's idea about an ethic of caring and love is one that is dependent on a natural feeling of care that instinctually drives human beings and is focused upon the response of the other party.

While I can appreciate the focus on relationship that Noddings makes central to her arguments, it is assumptive to suggest that everyone is endowed with a certain sense of caring. This poses a particular problem for women since it naturalizes the idea that the emotional responses of caring and love are feminine and maternal in nature and all women are innately designed to exude it. Those who don't are punished (see Grumet 1988; Luttrell 1997; Walkerdine 1990). While this suggests a skewed universal experience for the category of women, it is ironic that only the females from Collective Energy had no trouble with acknowledging their performances as both loving and political. Whose definition of caring is being used here? If we all have grown up with a variety of experiences that have been grouped under the umbrella of love and named as acts of "caring" despite their differences or even, as hooks (2000) pointed out earlier, their abusive nature, then the logic that suggests there is no discipline required to practice love or that there is no learning curve to the process of loving is unstable. Perhaps what is needed is a space to discuss what love could mean and what it is to make decisions that are rooted in love. Providing a method to explore love is another function of performance.

Performance provides the site where ideas about love and ethics can be explored in a useful way. Performance can offer us ways to practice a love ethic because it opens up space to cultivate the practice of revelation: exploring and revealing a more honest self and, more importantly, exposing the dynamics of relationship that shape the discourses through which we recognize love and are recognized as loving and lovable. It opens us up to practices that enable us to choose our responses while maintaining the "capacity to invent our lives . . . and we practice this shape-shifting to cope with unjust realities that cannot be easily changed" (hooks 2000, 57). Perceiving love in the way hooks describes here means accepting that performance and the concept of love are political. They are acknowledged and recognized as acts of community rather than those of an individual self—they are about maximizing moments of connection with self and with other. How we love and how we perform our selves is directly reflected in how we act out love and the performance of our selves in relation to others.

In order to experiment and explore the issues of love and responsibility, the practice of "inventing our lives" that hooks (2000) speaks of requires that we imagine how we wish our lives to be. Marnina Gonick (2003) suggests that the space of the imagination

> grants a certain license from the constraints of the social, the dictates of censorship, and other normative operations of consciousness. In the realm of the imaginary it may be possible to explore fantasies and fears, enact relations that would otherwise be restricted if not taboo, or temporarily dissolve boundaries, facilitating a loss of distinctiveness of the border between self and other. (182)

The motion made permissible by the utilization of the imaginary allows for experimentation, so that even if we have not been taught to love by our families or a society that has hurt us and themselves, or one that simply didn't know how to love, we may still have the space and time to practice and figure out what it means to love. hooks (2000) agrees: "What we cannot imagine cannot come into being," and it is performance that provides the opportunity to explore our imagined relations, desires, and in-between of our imaginations (14). The occasion that performance provides to rehearse these relations allows us to practice meaning what we say and doing what we mean, effectively turning our insides out. The safety net in the midst of these risky acrobatics is that we never have to perform the same way twice—in fact, it's pretty impossible to do so. An exploration of performance as the practice of love ethic and as a site of negotiation that is often overlooked in the mainstream "may make possible the imagining of new modes of life, provoking a disruption of conventional thought and action, inciting desire for and engendering strange possibilities extending the range of identities . . . others might negotiate" (Gonick 2003, 182). Using performance, we can constantly rehearse and recreate our imagination, thus adding to the repertoire of subjectivities and shifts in relationship that are available to us now. Performance space and the conversation space provided by purposefully structured workshops, such as Collective Energy's meetings, are crucial to this practice until it becomes an expectation that everyone is subject to change. These moments of meeting and connection become moments of transformation. So does performance.

hooks (2000) argues that the practice of loving is transformative, stating, "Commitment to a love ethic offers us a new set of values to live by" (88). She continues, "When love is present the desire to dominate and exercise power cannot rule the day" (98). This ethic of love and care is never far from the center of a socially responsible artist's creative push; according to Carol Becker (2001), "Artists care about society, enough to put their bodies on the line" (107). Two interesting elements underlie these statements. First, both of those quotes assume that to care is to sacrifice. The artist is risking her body, and the lover is deferring power. Second, when love informs ethical practices, transformation takes place and is evident through everyday life. The interest of the individual self is displaced or subsumed in service to others, and the artist initiates a transaction between self and audience by giving the self as an offering.

I pause here and think of the students in Collective Energy. I think of the stories they've shared and of the large quantities of time we spent together—that is another vital ingredient in an ethic of love—devotion of time.

During my work on this text, I was invited to Toronto to perform with some of my dear friends and, if I may, two of the most well-respected poets in North America; the show was organized by Toronto-based poet and impresario Dwayne Morgan, and we were relaxing backstage with another guest poet, New York City's Carlos Andrés Gómez. We were in the dressing room, waiting for the show to start, and I was picking their brains about love and about what it meant to them as artists. Dwayne, straight faced and unblinking, said that love was a choice, an irrational and passionate choice. Carlos said that love was about letting go. Their responses surprised me, and I worked to apply them to the feedback I received from Collective Energy. If love meant sacrifice, then understanding a performance as sacrifice was not hard to do. The artist was committing everything, submitting to the interpretation of the audience, presenting their embodied work, letting go like Carlos said. Dwayne's definition of love as a choice made me think that love had to be both—the artist was choosing to sacrifice.

The delicate work of locating the individual autonomous self/selves within the community of humanity (and vice versa) is all too often clumsily plodded through or simplistically addressed. What this work *requires*, however, is interaction between others and selves and recognition of the validity of that in-between space where such interaction occurs. Careful attention to this process is the ultimate demand of an ethics of embodiment, for any knowledge produced by a collective body is produced under very particular circumstances. This process requires respect and honesty. Such vigilance also requires a lifestyle commitment.

Another question that might be asked, particularly with the interest of artistic creation in mind, is what sorts of boundaries does this version of ethics lay for what is assumed to be a limitless imagination? The imagination is, as Gonick (2003) states, a traditionally excluded site of discourse that can be used to "challenge normative social and discourse practices—then the work of the imaginary seems a means of accessing and mining these excluded sites and other selves for what they might offer in the way of expansions of human capacity and social forms" (182). Or, as Lorri Neilsen Glenn (2008) writes, it is "our capacity to imagine [that] gives shape and direction to how we, as a species, learn from one another and transform our experience" (xv). If hooks's (2000) love ethic is combined with these other versions of imaginative possibility and the careful research and practice of embodiment and a/r/tography, then we are looking at an ethical relationship that requires a thorough examination and honest acknowledgment of power operations. Therefore, this ethics must welcome the unknown and be "centered on action aimed at subverting hegemonic relationships" (Jagger as in Springgay 2008, 156). The crux of our work holds a specific attention to the in-between, or to the gaps in order to better seek out and explore the moments when "there is a gap between the values [we] claim to hold and [our] willingness to do the work of connecting thought and action, theory and practice to realize these values and thus create a more just society" (hooks 2000, 90).

Collective Energy was an invitation to those of us participating to learn new ways to stand up effectively for the first time as artists. It was also the first time many of us stood up knowing that we had the support, if not the agreement, of eight others behind us. Performing original work provided this group of artists a way to audition our beliefs so that when we encountered moments of ethical decision making that occurred on or off the stage, we had practice behaving based out of a love ethic. Working to build a community of artists propelled us into intentional relationships with one another. Living through a feminist ethic of love enhances moments of contradictory experience, it "creates lived experiences together" and "nurture[s] . . . ethical relationality" through challenging and constantly revising those relationships (Springgay, 2008, 157). hooks (2000) agrees that "living ethically ensures that relationships in our lives, including encounters with strangers, nurture our spiritual growth" (88). This is the power behind an experience grown from love, invested in social responsibility and intentionally designed to point out and perform difference so that we can connect. This ethic of love requires social responsibility, and this conscientious attention is paid to our very being: "Our subjectivities, identities and ways of living in the world are gestures and situations that struggle with, contest, challenge, provoke, and embody an ethics of understanding and a responsibility" (Irwin and Springgay 2008, xxxii). Research, teaching, and performance cannot be siphoned off and acted out separately from one another, from values and ethics, or from the context that surrounds and scribes the artist. There is no way to separate who we are from what we do. Instead, "responsibility itself resides in the in-between," within and among these relationships we share (xxxii). So does love.

5

Been Around the World

After the year of writing, performing, and rehearsing together, Collective Energy concluded with a cultural immersion trip to the University of West Indies, St. Augustine campus, in Trinidad and Tobago. For several of the student artists, this trip was their first outside of the United States. For some, it was also their first time traveling on an airplane. For all of them, it was their first performance experience as an artist in the context of another country. Despite the various levels of familiarity each member brought to bear on the show, the broader context of international performance raises several important considerations for the socially responsible artist—particularly one that is coming from a Western perspective and entering communities with minimal context and expectation. My work as an artist and an activist continues to draw me outside the country on a regular basis, and I use this final chapter to probe the politics of spoken word poetry performance in an international setting. In the same way that hip hop has become globalized and yet returns to the United States, spoken word poetry has followed a similar path. What is the scope and scale of spoken word poetry's impact on socially responsible art production in regions of the Diaspora? How does spoken word poetry create moments of learning and invite international transactions of critical engagement and to what end? How has this performance technique continued to evolve as it becomes increasingly transnational? How might it function as a means of social transformation in different locations throughout the world? Looking toward Eastern Africa, specifically Tanzania, and the Caribbean context of Trinidad and Tobago, I use this chapter to offer examples of artists in action who inspire and energize a movement of socially responsible performance poetry that is worldwide.

In the Beginning Was the Word

The magnetism for producing hip hop and spoken word poetry lies not only in the examples they provide for scholarly analysis or in their accessibility by the masses—I am most compelled by their orientation toward action (Endsley 2013). As Tony's poem stated earlier, "words have power," and to speak words is to recreate power relationships that have the ability to upset the illusion of social harmony that is so easy to hum along with (Brookes 1992). To perform is to explicitly critique and expand the partial and multiple perspectives reiterated by mainstream media in the interest of maintaining social hierarchy. Because of the communication barriers that are often the first causes of friction between cultures, it's important to return to the two key aspects of language as a construction of power and performance as an embodied practice. Language is the foundational tool of the socially conscious spoken word artist who seeks to challenge oppressive discourses and stories that so often subdue any alternative telling of history. Using language to insist on equal rights, to disarm violence, and to write resistance is nothing new to women, especially all over the continent of Africa, who have been diligently working with one another to end various forms of patriarchy for years (see Browdy de Hernandez et al. 2010 for an excellent example). Stories that have been designated as coming from "the margins" when in fact they are central to the lives of many women across the Diaspora are being talked about, responded to, and are garnering attention within academe. Author Edwidge Danticat has published prolifically about her birthplace of Haiti and uses her pen to pierce holes in Western assumptions and generalizations by demonstrating the powerful healing that is possible through storytelling about women who come from the island. Danticat (2010) has this to say about her personal motivation for writing and specifically sharing the stories with Haitian roots:

> The immigrant artist shares with all other artists the desire to interpret and possibly remake his or her own world. So though we may not be creating as dangerously as our forebears—though we are not risking torture, beatings, execution, though exile does not threaten us into perpetual silence—still, while we are at work bodies are littering the streets somewhere . . . and still, many are reading, and writing, quietly, quietly. (p 18)

Danticat positions the acts of reading and writing as dangerous and creative—two adjectives that from a Western perspective, particularly within our educational system, are not immediately associated with literacy any longer. She also states that the desire of all artists is to "interpret and possibly remake [their] own world," and for an artist, that world includes his or her audience. According to Danticat, the writer is a pedagogue and the world is her student. This desire to interpret and share a revision of the world as the artist sees it is dependent upon a public audience. The teacher needs the student. We create—in spite of the threat of danger that is still imminent in certain areas around the globe, *because* of the bodies littering the streets, *because* of the policy that puts them there, *because* of looming fear, *because* of the injustice, the oppression, the struggle. We create—because of the bizarre experience of finding pleasure in the midst of this overwhelming depression. We create to connect, align, and disengage. And we are artists because we want to share a new vision with the world so that the world may understand that it has been remade, that it is changed, that it is different, and that we have done it.

Critical consideration for the undertakings and analyses offered by these groundbreaking feminist writers centers the overarching focus within my research of performance for several reasons. These are writers who are interested in the ways that writing and sharing stories join the reader and author to one another through forging a new connection the past, asking them to locate themselves in the present, and projecting a future after learning the tales. These writers contribute to what English and Black feminist scholar Elaine Richardson (2006) names the "discourse of Black consciousness" which prioritizes formal education and ancestral, everyday knowledge (1). Authors like Danticat and Chimamanda Ngozi Adichie (2007) align smoothly to feminist theorists such as Chandra Talpade Mohanty (2003) and Linda Tuhiwai Smith (1999) because they provide us with a specific perspective that consistently implicates the reader through calling up the social location of the author within their stories. These women demonstrate the power of using written text to focus on ignored lives and experiences, pushing them into our public social consciousness and thus countering the frequently reiterated, often irresponsible, and yet easily digested views of rheumy Western eyes. Mohanty (2003) posits a useful view of the concept of "solidarity," which I apply to the performance of spoken word poetry as it relates to moving across and within transnational contexts. She states:

> I define solidarity in terms of mutuality, accountability, and the recognition of common interests as the basis for relationships among diverse communities. Rather than assuming an enforced commonality of oppression, the practice of solidarity foregrounds communities of people who have chosen to work and fight together. Diversity and difference are central values here—to be acknowledged and respected, not erased in the building of alliances. (7)

Mohanty's vision for solidarity reverses the potentially paralyzing effects of realizing just how far apart lived experiences can be, especially as an American artist entering communities in different parts of the world. These women and girls have faced struggles I have only read about—again, they force me to ask, Who do I think I am? However, Mohanty's statement encourages an approach to transnational spoken word poetry performance opportunities with a goal that is motivated neither by some warped desire for "sameness" nor by a quest for comfort or pity. Instead, this method of engagement is driven by an action-oriented objective of solidarity and common interests, one that bands and bonds us in working and fighting on the same side. Mohanty's definition *values* difference; in fact, we are made more effective because of our uniqueness and the varied capabilities pushed to the foreground by performing identity work that is rooted in our lives. Approaching transnational performance through this lens enables me to be more aware and less afraid, alleviating the pressure of sameness and generalization that Western versions of White feminism so often encourages that we maintain, especially in the academy. Difference is not shushed or excluded, nor is it worshipped and exoticized. In my experience as both an artist and an academic, and a mixed-race woman within the context of Collective Energy as a leader and example for how to function in all of these capacities, finding the room to participate in each of these spheres matters to me. On a larger scale, my spoken word performance, through assessing and rehearsing under a socially responsible and feminist perspective, is imbued with a new ability in each new environment. Spoken word poetry performance calls attention to my competing subjectivities, and, by acknowledging them, makes room for them all to abide in correlation to those of the audience member. When the artist understands this possibility, and the accountability that accompanies it, they are able to enter into performance events, taking up identity as a source of knowledge as well as a basis for progressive collective action and mobility (Mohanty 2003, 6). Thus, the work of these women offers an anchor for my own feminist application of performance standards for spoken word poetry in an international context: although I have limited control over which direction the audience may steer what we coproduce, I am still held partially responsible for the outcome. I pay tribute to these writers and scholars because of their insistence on the centrality of identity when learning and teaching about and among communities other than my own. Also, written words are major components of spoken word poetry's ultimate performance; therefore it makes sense to point to those who write, and write with specific motivation, for a broad audience. There are two different examples that I reference to briefly in this chapter, each one limited in highlighting a few of the ways in which the art of spoken word poetry performances are used toward an effective and lasting empowerment within the Diaspora.

Tanzania

Tony and I had been in Arusha, Tanzania, for about four weeks. Nearly cold at night, but warm with zero humidity in the daytime, mornings were clear and quiet—my favorite part of the day. I learned to look for the smoke rising in a pillar from the stove by the kitchen building because that meant the water would be hot in the shower. The students that were a part of the class we were assisting with fried our nerves and burrowed our friendship with one another even deeper. The generosity of the community astounded us. One of my most salient memories was being invited for chai—a word for tea, mostly milk, very sweet and cinnamon flavored—and chapatti—a simple flat bread made of flour, oil, and salt that accompanied most meals—one afternoon by a young man named Kwele who was also interested in music production and had a love for hip hop and for his community. As we walked over to where he lived, my throat burned with the knowledge that he was willing to sacrifice in order to treat me to tea. I was a complete stranger who, although at home was labeled as a poor student on food stamps, had more tins of food in my kitchen at home than his cupboards would see in a month. I felt convicted on a spiritual level, for my privilege, for my birthplace. Yet he would go without so that I could have something extra. I wouldn't think of insulting him by turning him down, and I calmed myself by figuring out a way to exchange the hospitality: I left him with the music CDs I had brought with me on the trip. That afternoon's tea was vibrant—peppered with plenty of hand gestures on my part and laughs on his, we shared ideas, questions, thoughts about music, poetry, life. His kindness humbled me. I felt I had made a friend. Back on site I tried to explain to Tony what I was feeling and I began to cry. I was betrayed by my body, the stories my skin and hair told without giving me a chance to explain who I was and that I too was looking for home. Despite this and without ever mentioning race or social standing or even gender, Kwele offered me the respect of listening intently to my thoughts and ideas. I remember asking Tony, what is it that we are really doing here? What is it that we think we have to offer? Were we taking more than we gave?

Tony and I had worked to adjust to the new environment: temperature, the time difference, and the learning of greetings and small talk in Swahili. The toilets and the modes of travel were even becoming less awkward to us.

Our first time to Tanzania and we jumped in head first. We had been leading poetry workshops in the community center with a range of children who brought joy to the classroom that propelled us into digging deeper to keep them engaged and to offer something new and exciting. We were tired. We were thrilled. I was there when Tony recorded in the music studio, for the first time ever and in Tanzania no less, and he was there when I was called upon to perform at the Community Concert with hip hop artists from Kenya and Dar es Salaam. The afternoon of the concert while the stage and equipment were being set up we were mingling with the artists as they began to trickle down to the center. The engineer and host for the night's show was making introductions to one particular MC, and I said hello. The MC looked me up and down without a word before turning to Tony. Reaching for dap from Tony, the MC asked "What's up nigga?" And just like that, this word we hadn't heard the entire time, living in a place where our foreignness had less to do with skin color than with the social class and privilege associated with being American, we were propelled backward. Tony dapped the MC, a Black African who hailed from Nairobi, but said nothing. Turning to me, he spoke as if the wind had been knocked out of him. "I'll be right back." I was flooded with anger even as my mind assessed the reasons why that had been the phrase this MC used to greet Tony. And I could list every reason that Tony walked away, stunned.

We were participating as assistants to the first ever service-learning trip coordinated through the Women's Studies department on campus, and the title of the course was "Arts as Global Activism." The destination was Arusha, Tanzania, on the eastern coast of Africa. This trip was similar to Collective Energy's experience in Trinidad and Tobago for a couple of reasons. For many of the students participating, the trip to Arusha was their first time traveling outside of the United States' borders. I had traveled abroad with two of the members of the class: Alyssa and Tony. I was thrilled to have their company on this journey as well. This was also a course that utilized the arts as global activism focusing on community empowerment—but that is where the similarities ended.

Members of the class included a larger group of students, over twenty-five, accompanied by multiple faculty members and guided by assistants like Tony and myself. Of the group, only four of us were people of color, and everyone else was White. None of us had ever been anywhere in Africa prior to this trip, and none of us were fluent in Kiswahili. Also, the travel portion of the class grew from a structured on-campus course; we spent two weeks predeparture in summer school meeting for long hours of class every day and then spent four additional weeks on site overseas. We were hosted by the

United African Alliance Community Center (UAACC) in Arusha, located at the foot of Mt. Meru, in Imbaseni Village. The UAACC was founded by former leader of the Black Panther Party Pete O'Neal and his beautiful and artistically talented wife, Charlotte. The story of how the UAACC came to be in existence is potent, and a documentary called *A Panther in Africa*, directed by Aaron Matthews (2005), provides significant underpinnings about the founding and current mission of the UAACC. During our time, the class traveled to Masai land, went on safari, and hiked the lower portion of Mt. Kilimanjaro. Tanzania is an astounding place filled with rich history and culture, and my colleague, Dr. Marla Jaksch, who coordinated this course, continues her collaborative activist research projects with women across Tanzania and Zanzibar. Her work persists in inspiring me. Ever since this initial trip, I have returned almost annually to perform and participate in as many broad ways as possible with Marla and the communities she works with. Marla chose Arusha, Tanzania, as the destination for this initial course because of her introduction to Charlotte and Pete O'Neal. Mzee Pete (a respectful title in Swahili—it's almost like addressing Pete as grandfather) and Mama C (Charlotte's stage name, and again "mama" is a respectful title for an older woman in the community) continue to do tremendous work in Imbaseni and beyond. Mama C returns to the United States every year for a tour, promoting the mission of the UAACC, showcasing her incredible visual art, and lately playing and singing with her band. She is also well known in the artistic community in Eastern Africa, Zanzibar in particular. Mama C's generous spirit makes her well loved, and her warm demeanor and the fluent Swahili she speaks still hold traces of the Kansas City accent that reminds her listener where she was raised. After our initial visit to Tanzania, Tony and I had the good fortune of hosting Mama C during a Collective Energy workshop meeting. She was visiting Penn State as part of her Heal the Community tour and her art was on exhibit at our campus. We were so honored to have Mama C visit us accompanied by Marla. Collective Energy's weekly meetings created a space that invited the teaching and learning of a global aesthetic even before we traveled abroad.

By the point that Mama C visited with us, this bond was well established and she slid easily into our existing group dynamic. Our time with her profoundly impacted our scope of understanding what was possible through arts performance. She was a tangible example of how poetry and performance could impact an entire city and fuel worldwide tours. Her eagerness to share her expertise was not lost on Collective Energy. Mama C shared some of her poetry and provided insightful commentary and feedback on the work of the student artists. It was an evening not to be forgotten. Here was a woman who, after the turbulent time of the 1960s, had relocated to Africa, enduring tribulations that we had only read about. And now Mama C uses her role as an artist to raise global awareness and funding to address her new community's social issues. Mama C provides a shining example of the ways an artist can cross boundaries and create positive change simultaneously in the United States and in East Africa. While she calls Arusha home, she has not neglected the community that raised her in the United States, and she endeavors to nurture new bonds through each performance she gives no matter the location.

The time that Tony and I spent in Tanzania for the six-week course we were assisting with provided an abundance of entryways into discussions about the concept of service learning, community, activism, and education. However, I focus here on those two tender memories that manifest both the theory of spoken word poetry performance as activism and the dual roles of artist and audience. Performance is the spoken word artist's method of teaching, making visible these alternatives and centralizing a political critique of injustice. In his pioneering work on performance theory and the governing state in East Africa, Ngũgĩ wa Thiong'o reminds us that performances "acquire their real power only in relationship to the audience" (1997, 12). There is intense competition for this limited amount of power that Thiong'o attributes to the legacy of colonialism, yet it is from the midst of this tension that a performance artist can potentially have a deep and lasting impact on an audience, and therefore a community.

The socially responsible spoken word artist thus poses a threat to any social institution that seeks to silence and disenfranchise the audience of the artist. Because many spoken word audiences and practicing artists are young people of color, this situates these demographics in direct opposition to most major forms of government and acting authority members of the state. The success and support of spoken word poetry performances relies on the participation of their audience members to coconstruct the stories and knowledge that are reproduced and performed. Because of this two-way interdependent relationship, the site of spoken word poetry performances becomes disputed ground for struggles of power and agency (see Endsley 2014). There are equal amounts of risk and responsibility undergirding each performance of spoken word poetry, and these vulnerabilities are exponentially increased during an international performance. The relationship between artist and audience member becomes even more critical when the performer is from the United States and the audience is in East Africa. Like the palimpsests of old, layers upon layers of history and power and privilege coat each performance, revealing meanings as they are removed and communicating desires as they are added. The connection shared by audience and artist must be attended with supreme care at all times. This responsibility is magnified for both the artist and the audience in a global setting.

The spoken word artist seeks to unify and mobilize and at the same time defragment the assumptions and privilege that scribe life "in the West." Simultaneously, it is a dangerous game to assume that an audience consisting of people with limited exposure to Black and Brown life in America will critically consume a performance production by live artists inhabiting these subjectivities. Bakari Kitwana (2004) has suggested that hip hop artists have earned the right to explore the ideals of freedom and democracy assumed by the identity of being American, and that in so doing "we feel the innate right to loose the chains of being and knowing, including definitions of race" (115). In the same way that hip hop artists have used their agency to create subversion and perform multiple interpretations of what it means to be Black and Brown in the borders of America, spoken word artists have the potential to perform in such a way that also emphasizes the multiple and communal meanings that are implicit in performance (Bost 2001). In other words, spoken word poetry that is socially responsible in a transnational setting acknowledges the problematic hierarchy that privileges certain embodied identities and employs an awareness that those identities that afforded privilege and power shift dramatically depending upon the geographic location. The spoken word artist then critiques the very identities she performs by calling them up and newly appropriating them in multiple ways toward a goal of producing new knowledges. Art of all types can be designed to shake up coagulated beliefs and practices that fail to address the conflict of being "of color" and American, a lover and a fighter, a critic and a patriot.

Putting Words in My Mouth

From Arusha to the capital city of Dar es Salaam in Tanzania, hip hop music has cleared a path for the intersection and boomeranging arc of cultural invention that reconnects the practice and preservation of oral history in the United States back to African roots. Murray Forman (2011) refers to Africa as "ground zero, the original site of the drum and dance from which hip hop was born" (Forman in Saucier 2011, xi). While Hip Hop certainly follows in the tradition of jazz, blues, and rock 'n' roll as specifically Black American inventions, there is no doubt that tribute must be paid to the heritage of aesthetics passed down and then remixed within each generation and social movement, resulting in the contemporary expressive elements of the culture. At the same time, because of the nuances specific to the practices within each locale and social position across the globe, the inventiveness and multiplicity of remixes taken up by youth invested in social change are incredibly versatile. These characteristics of hip hop in general and within the context of Tanzania specifically are key to understanding the ways in which spoken word poetry performance also takes up similar causes and suffers the same opposition from a different approach. Hip hop across Africa accounts for new exposure to old problems of police brutality, poverty, and imperialism, for example, that continue to plague youth across the globe: the very practice of hip hop is the contradiction that so many youth face. At once there is the space to deconstruct the social oppression and identities that young bodies are inscribed with, and at the same time, hip hop functions as a means to simply reproduce narratives of oversimplified materialism and violence or to push social and political propaganda (Brennan, Burton, and Lawi 2007; Saucier 2011; Ntarangwi 2009). Broadly speaking, Kitwana's (2004) reminder that there is more than one way to perform Blackness and Brownness and that hip hop culture is an ideal place to audition these performances extends an invitation to the audience to partake in a remix of their own (Endsley 2012). The either/or binary is played out, a tired script we've witnessed and acted upon repeatedly, and yet it is one that ever-presently shapes the relationships of contemporary American politics and global relations.

This confused language, heavy with power and clumsy in the delicate work of relationship building is what bruised Tony and me in the introduction to the Kenyan MC at the beginning of this section of the chapter. Although we were all performing artists using very similar creative tools to address similar social issues, that did not make up for the lack of understanding or education around the history of American slavery, of inequality and racism that pervasively acts out its drama and abuse through language in the United States. That strife was too much to attempt to explain that night, only moments before we were to take the stage. The fact was that this MC, with zero understanding and consciousness of what harm he had just inflicted, sliced through the grand notions we had of making any sort of difference in another country. I use that exchange as an example of exactly how powerful language is and how in an instant that power can shift, destabilizing expectations and desires. Nuance and shared history were suddenly irrelevant. We felt the burdensome weight of realization that no matter how well we performed or the number of encores we received during that concert, our distant relatives perceived the unknown, young,

Black American male body as a nigger because hip hop instructed them that doing so was acceptable and expected. Our disconnect with each other on a micro-scale was clear instantly but a way to address it was not. Just because we fought on the same side against massive social problems using performance did not mean we shared the same goals and history.

Perhaps home was not home at all. Even when not on stage, working within the setting of East Africa in particular externalized a loss of power that Tony and I had come to grips with as natural: Tony was an African American, a Black male body, and had little to do with the decision-making processes that scribed his existence in urban America. In Tanzania, even as an invited guest artist and instructor, we were again stripped of any say in how we were reacted to. Although in the broader picture we enjoyed systemic privileges and social status, in the intimate moments of trying to negotiate relationship with other respected artists who were more well known and held authority at the concert event, we were declined admittance. All of the beauty and anticipation of performing was dulled in that single exchange. Yet, as we took the stage that night, spoken word poetry was a means to reclaim a position that refused the generic void we had been assigned. Performing allowed us to write another layer into the readings of our embodied existence. We had a chance to speak out and against the parts of ourselves that had been denied us.

Encounters like this one exemplify why, in a conversation about contemporary spoken word poetry, it is imperative to address the continued momentum and heavy influence of the hip hop movement on the continent. Frequently, the same practitioners and supporters of hip hop are the benefactors of spoken word poetry as well. In my experience, spoken word poetry is often grouped together with hip hop MCs in Tanzanian performance venues or concerts without much delineation being made between the two. The question I am asked without fail after I come off stage in Tanzania is: "Have you ever thought about adding the drum behind your words?" Suggestions that I add music give dimension to the expected practices of cultural producers within this context as well as the aesthetic standards that many audience members subscribe to. They don't introduce me as a poet or a spoken word artist—I'm an MC that "freestyles." In the same way it draws from hip hop, spoken word poetry also recalls the legacy of the griots that were relied upon for the genealogy and memory of entire communities and the powerful role they play in African history. Relating historical fact and myth to contemporary politics and debates is a responsibility of a griot as well; similarly spoken word poetry functions to insert the same concerns and realities of youth into a global narrative (Endsley 2012). The overlaps between the role of the griot and the hip hop MC provide a fruitful ground for spoken word poetry to function effectively as a tool for political critique and identity formation as well as art for social change. As performed in a transnational setting, whether by an artist from the West in the heart of Tanzania or a figure such as Mama C returning to the states as a stranger in her old home, spoken word poetry is crucial in navigating multiple local identities within global representations.

As always, the subversion of a dominant discourse is tricky—if a performer from the United States isn't careful, she may simply reiterate and bury the very power relations she seeks to expose. I find Thiong'o's (1997) explanation of the pedagogical exchange that transpires within performance in a specifically East African context very useful:

> The community learned and passed its moral codes and aesthetic judgments through narratives, dances, theatre, rituals, music, games, and sports. With the emergence of the state, the artist and the state become not only rivals in articulating the laws, moral or formal, that regulate life in society, but also rivals in determining the manner and circumstances of their delivery. (11)

According to Thiong'o's statement, the community is implicated as responsible for what transpires during and after a performance, for it is the community who polices behaviors and choices, deeming some acceptable and desirable and others as socially immoral. This is key in understanding the call-and-response relationship of shared accountability between artist and audience. While Thiong'o points to the predominant struggles between the discourses of state and artist on a nationalist scale, let's turn for a moment to the management of conduct that is determined by the community through the artist's performance.

For example, if a spoken word artist invokes the specific and opposing discourses that may reflect the experiences of a young Black man from an urban area in America through a performance, they are enacting and reenacting identities. Some of these identities are easily recognizable to an audience who is exposed to mostly mainstream media and news. There might be expectations of wealth, power, and privilege, as well as lack of education, violence, and offensive language scribed onto the same artist's body. If the identities showcased in a performance instead conflict with perpetuated stereotypes or generalized experiences unfamiliar to the audience, the spoken word artist can both utilize and supersede the common operating system by revising the identities he or she might otherwise be limited to performing when off stage. This brave act on behalf of the artist encourages a similar destabilization by the audience. Because hip hop, and therefore spoken word poetry by association of the elements, is often *only* recognized or acknowledged by the media and mainstream culture by its commodified and neatly packaged appearances, there is often a disconnect that erupts in their Diasporic contexts: Tony's introduction is an example of such a clash. While the spread of hip hop and spoken word poetry has been gaining international ground since their inception, the political roots grounding these cultural movements aren't always brought to the forefront for the listener who comprises their global counterparts much like in America.

Unfortunately, the same way the Top 40 radio rotation exposes the general public to a very small and selectively chosen slice of hip hop tracks, the same is true for the spread of hip hop to East Africa. Part of the appeal and complicated practice of the culture is that these contradictions are engaged with, employed, and explored in such a way that endangers some and excites others. This is why an analysis of these intimate moments of contact have much to offer us in terms of the promise of innovative moments of agency that occur for young people in spite of constraints and limitations imposed by external factors. This is messy work. There is no singular and tidy integration of the artistic offspring of spoken word poetry or hip hop after each performance encounter. Kitwana (2004) cautions that "we should draw distinctions between the various cultural ideas that converge as hip-hop has become a staple of American popular culture. Black popular culture is not a carbon copy of hip-hop culture" (115). This is one component of the sophisticated equation of production and consumption of culture. Relationships become increasingly complicated as the layers are added and erased, bolded and italicized depending on who is reading, writing, and performing and ultimately where and when the interaction takes place.

The need for distinction between cultures, aims, and goals of socially responsible art, along with careful analyses of specific performances, is crucial now more than ever. With the onset of the Internet, YouTube sensations and social media allow for an ever-increasing flow of information and consumption—and while this is exciting because of the wild variety of cross-pollination made available at our fingertips, many of our people lack the skills to critically consume and produce this culture. So whether the information or representations of people of color be correct, false, healthy, or deadly to the communities that are up for discussion online or through recorded albums, they are available. While the market has expanded mightily, providing access to the tools for learning to synthesize and think critically about what images we see and hear lags sorely behind. Totalizing assumptions, generalizations, old racisms, and myths are circulated at a faster rate, and misconceptions about the poor, communities of color, and other oppressed demographics run more rampant than ever before. Public schools in the United States struggle to keep up with the latest technological trend at a time when resources and government funding are failing us. Admission into colleges grows increasingly competitive for all who apply, while learning and skill gaps resulting from poorly resourced schools and teachers in K–12 classrooms are exacerbated in the writing and reading basic skill levels of first-year college students. The crisis of public education combined with the abundance of accessible popular culture points to the essential need to train our minds to constantly interrogate what we are taught, how we are entertained, and at what cost. I am committed to conducting scholarly research about culture and simultaneously creating cultural performances because of my own investment in the power of education and my firsthand knowledge that using the arts can assist young people by providing opportunities for agency. Powerful moments of pedagogy are available when performance arts are used as a method of inquiry into the world and our roles in it. The very reason I believe that spoken word poetry performance is a fundamental part of social responsibility is because it depends upon that ever-present fifth element—knowledge of self. We know others through our relationship with them: they teach us who we are and who we are not. When these relational understandings are applied systemically within the current context of discourse, cultural production/consumption, and knowledge production, they shape how we function in the world. Through these discourses, each vying to be more popular and powerful than the others, we form our worldview. This view of the world determines the reception, response, and trajectory of social change for the artist and community audience in a transnational performance event.

Hip hop culture as promoted by a capitalist American business corporation is commodified, marketed, and sold with little thought given to synthesizing the political underpinnings of this commercial entity. As stated by Brad Porfilio and Michael Viola (2012) in their overview of the state of hip hop in a context of globalization:

> Over the past three decades, hip hop has become a site of contestation with a corporate music industry incredibly adept at redirecting hip hop's social energies away from critical expressions of struggle, protest, and resistance toward messages of materialism, greed, and individualism. The music that dominates the charts speaks to this shift with social messages propagating

> individualistic pursuits of extravagant cars, flashy jewelry, and stylish clothes . . . aligning more closely with White, male, corporate executives who promote a materialistic, misogynist, homophobic, and violent "gangsta image" of hip hop culture. (5; see also Dyson 1996; Porfilio and Carr 2010)

There is no shortage of socially responsible hip hop production—but the limited funds of underground artists often make access and radio play extremely difficult to come by, particularly when overseas. The result is a marginalization of the American hip hop artists who aren't included in the larger conversation of popular culture, thus the radical stories they spit are all too often drowned out by the blaring of chart-topping popular rap. This gap is exacerbated in an international context, and spoken word poetry is not far behind. It is not hard to trace much of the racist, misogynist, and classist dialogue that determines how youth are allowed and expected to "be" and the ways they are interacted with, yet mainstream media pays little attention to the remnant of hip hop heads and spoken word artists around the world that are mobilizing politically and taking concrete action to change the social climate through transformative artwork. Cultural movements remain a crucial site of intervention for theory and praxis. Resisting appropriation and maintaining creative control and integrity have become increasingly important and pose particular challenges through the differences that are illuminated when we cross borders. Here I want to focus on the hopeful possibilities that spoken word poetry can offer youth, educators, and artists who seek to engage and participate in a transformative fundamental shift in our campuses and in our streets.

The potential for social change within a specific spoken word poetry performance context offers us a new method that extends and deepens the approach that hip hop provides. Spoken word poetry performance is often pared down, without the distraction of music or much movement. Spoken word is energized because of the differences that are made visible for the artist and the audience member. To point out differences is to draw attention to similarities as well. Performance of spoken word poetry invokes a sense of "shared citizenship," and as the performance takes place, the audience member enters into the construction of the lived experience of the artist (Freire and Macedo 1993, 54). Once audience members become active participants, they too contribute in reconstructing the meanings of any given performance. Plural meanings and open-ended negotiations occur during each performance, which causes discourses to vie for power, question authority, and recede in an ongoing process—there is constant motion. The disruption and displacement of system-wide ideologies allow space for more divergent and fluid identities to be rehearsed, thereby deflating oppressive systems of belief in order to make room for new ideas. Performing the same content within two different contexts will always result in an entirely new performance because of what each audience member, location, and current events bring to bear on each show. This marks both parties as responsible for the circumstance that the experience is rooted in and commits them to enforcing or allowing that structure to exist and be perpetuated.

Performing spoken word poetry in a global context becomes an even more intensified reflective practice because the mirror is two-way: audience and artist must concurrently cross-examine one another as well as their own subjectivity. Freire (2000) reminds us that to achieve any hope of change, we must remain committed to the transformation of word into action and back again, ensuring a constant shift between reflection and activism (88). To create the space and momentum required by social change, we must attend to the relationship between the words we use and the actions we take—it is not enough to take action for action's sake, nor will it satisfy our goals to merely talk (88). Freire's work addresses the ongoing upkeep of critical theorizing and pedagogy, and I suggest that because of spoken word poetry's reliance on the word as well as the performance, this form of cultural production is prime material for such a practice. Again, relationship is at the center of this dimension of critical thinking and production.

In order to address the links between localized pedagogical practices and performance as transformation, I look to Ngũgĩ wa Thiong'o's (1986) extensive work, which insists that the only way "to control a people's culture is to control their tools of self-definition in relationship to others" (16). How we define the other is how we define ourselves: this is the way we learn what we are and are not, who we have permission to become, and why. Spoken word poetry in an international setting works to charge the artist and audience through the synapses of these connections and to make us aware of the gaps in our understanding. Because spoken word poetry is so fluid, its performance challenges rigid notions of identity and dichotomy. The spoken word artist and the audience members use the moment of performance to cocreate how they view one another and how they might reimagine the world, making performance very much a living, evolving occurrence. Negotiating meanings during each performance then equips audience members to return to their localized situation with fresh understandings of worldwide historical moments and their impact. This transaction and transition both complicates and opens up new considerations for the political and social decisions that are entered into in daily life.

Performance is exciting precisely because it is so unstable and decentralizing: there is no singular appropriate reaction. Instead, multiple directions and configurations are generated in each performance moment, swelling into the momentum of a movement. Because of this influence and impact, the spoken word performance is politicized, marking the artist as a potential threat to the state and capitalist economy. Within these moments of performance, the artist and audience find tools and techniques of resistance, calls for accountability and responses of responsibility: this is the art of protest.

The sun was setting on New Year's Eve. An outdoor festival on the white sands of Zanzibar with a full moon eager to show herself even before the sun had said a proper good night. Tony and I had been invited to spit as the opening performances for a three-day arts festival. Mama C and her band were to feature later on in the evening after the crowd had been warmed up. Here we were again, sharing the stage that was sometimes gracious and other times silent with apathy at our words. Years had passed since our introduction to Tanzania's varied landscape, and our encounters were sometimes polite and generous and other times threatened us with the sharp teeth of hatred. Before we took the stage, our backs to smooth ocean waters, our eyes on that full moon, Tony grabbed my hand. "Dada, I can't believe we get to do this." Squeezing his hand back, I shook my head, insides full to bursting. "Let them have it," I whispered. "Let them have it all."

Trinidad and Tobago

"Fix ya middle!!" Alyssa screams amid whoops of laughter as we poured out of the blazing hot van. We had been begging our new friends Marvin and poet Muhammed to teach us Trini slang. He obliged with a smile. To tell someone to fix their middle was to instruct them to get it together and to stop letting their personal business hang all out for the world to see. It's something akin to calling someone "messy" in the United States. After a late night of choking back puncheon—a liquor beverage that will bring tears to your eyes—at a local bar and eating doubles—delicious pastry stuffed with curry-seasoned meat and vegetables—from a street vendor, we were ready to hit the legendary beaches. Although we were on spring break from school, thus far we had been diligently attending workshops and soaking up the vibrant history of the beautiful island since our arrival. Our full-length show wasn't until the end of the week, and we were ready for some downtime and relaxation. I had unwittingly assumed that because the group of student artists was small there would be a bit less

pressure on me during the trip—wrong again, Crys. Because our group was so small, any shift in emotion or tension quickly became evident to everyone, and I was feeling the stress of wanting to let go and enjoy myself versus biting my tongue and being a responsible administrator of a cultural program. But for this afternoon in particular, we were beside ourselves with excitement and giddy at the prospect of wearing only our swimsuits and enjoying the sun like the tourists we were. We were joined by a few other students from University of West Indies (UWI) we had met who couldn't resist our invitation to a beach day. The ride to the ocean front seemed to fly by, and we joked easily with one another and asked the driver to blare the music as loud as he was willing. As we came tumbling out of the van, I remember the first glimpse of the sun glinting off the ocean's surface, almost metallic. I felt a bit disoriented, not yet accustomed to flipping the switch of educator and program leader to just go to the beach like everyone else. It felt a bit backward to me, a premature celebration before the real work had been completed. I wanted to be finished with our show. I wanted the applause.

Grass like velvet and an invitation to perform. We were outside in the wide open of the UWI campus green and it was open mic night. The sound system carried the voices and rhythms of poets and vocalists across the expanse and even those seated on the picnic tables under the brick archway could hear clearly. The weather could not have felt better. There weren't even any mosquitoes out. Talk about a perfect cultural program—poetry, with the stars as decorations, rounded off with a live band for the interludes. Students were clumped together across the grass or standing in small groups murmuring so as not to interrupt those who had signed up on the list to perform. It was clear that this was a popular program at UWI just like our BED was back home, and yet the vibe was so different from what we were used to at Penn State. Mellow is the word that best describes the evening. Even with the performers that were fired up and passionate in their delivery style, their expressiveness was welcomed and then swallowed whole by the atmosphere. Maybe it was because we were outdoors. Each member of Collective Energy went up independently at some point during the evening and shared a piece from their repertoire. I was prouder than a rooster, practically strutting. Tears gathered in the corner of my eye. I helped to bring them here, to this point in their journey as artists, as students, as people. It is rare that as an educator or performing artist I am given the opportunity to witness tangible effects or results of the investments of time and energy I have sown in the lives of others. The demands of this job are high without much physical return. To be present at this performance, not even the principal show we still had yet to perform as a group, and to see each of these students stand on their own and rock with a crowd full of strangers made me choke up. I had done something good here. I had contributed to something worthwhile. After a few hours, the official program came to a close, folks were socializing, and several of the UWI students had come up to introduce themselves and talk with the members of Collective Energy. Without formal planning, we found ourselves standing in a circle, and a cypher had begun. Each of us went around the circle spitting poems, singing verses of songs, focused on attentive listening, feeling the contact high of building off of one another's energy. This was the conversation I had been listening for—the unscripted, organic response to each other's words and motivation. The cypher was the connection, and it continued on for several cycles before, just as easily as it had come together, it split apart.

The experience Collective Energy shared during the weeklong Cultural Immersion at the University of West Indies, St. Augustine, cemented our bond in ways that only the intensity of airline travel and living together in one house can. The conflicts that arose during that week were mostly due to adjusting to a completely new environment that none of us had previously experienced—and the particular challenges that rose in our roles as performing artists and guests. For example, all travel to and from the house we were staying in had to be done by vehicle with a local driver, and we couldn't travel anywhere alone or even walk by ourselves. Limited mobility while in a house full of excited folks, a packed schedule, having to navigate the sharing of bedrooms and bathrooms are all part and parcel of conducting a cultural program overseas. Toby had packed our itinerary, and we were excited about what each new day would bring. We were going to make the most of our time in St. Augustine, and the beautiful climate and delicious food helped me to be content in relinquishing most of the control that I had been struggling to balance while at home. There was yet a lesson for me to learn as a leader in this new territory.

Part of the reason Toby chose UWI as our partner institution was due to their Arts in Action program. In their graduate school, they offer a program that centralizes the use of art as a tool of social action, matriculating students through this program in order to equip them with the pedagogical theory as well as the technical skills to perform. The use of spoken word poetry was combined with theater practices in order to do so. One afternoon, we had a workshop that centered upon improvisational skills that demonstrated for Collective Energy how one of their neighborhood interventions might be formatted. We had the opportunity to participate in a training led by two of their instructors on campus including: brainstorming a topic or choosing a social issue to address, practicing interacting with unscripted dialogue, and imagining a variety of scenarios that may play out depending on the audience's reaction. We learned about the use of props, comedy, and the importance of being knowledgeable about the specific social history for each community that would serve as a performance site. Having this background could mean the difference in establishing dialogue or being shut out from the community. Since Collective Energy's show was coming up in this brand-new context for a brand-new audience, I remember wondering if we had done a thorough enough job of learning our audience's context. There seemed to be inevitable abrasion caused by performance no matter what the setting, and this troubled me. Clear differences stand out when comparing spoken word poetry performance like the type we had all participated in the night before at the outdoor open mic on campus and the sorts of "in-community" staged performances that we were being taught about in the campus workshop. Those differences, including the structure of each event, the artists' and the audience makeup, and the environment set the tone for the sort of interaction invited at the time of each show. However, friction was always present in the performance settings, and while I understood the energy that might result, it was also plain to see that the same rough scraping of discourse might just as quickly ignite into destructive flames. This conflict is to be expected during all enactments of power, but artists should expect the clash to be even sharper "where the state is externally imposed, in a situation where there is a conqueror and the conquered for instance, as in colonialism" (Thiong'o 1997, 12). Collective Energy was an invited guest at a very controlled performance venue taking place during an annual literary festival. Our audience mostly consisted of a few hundred young people who appeared excited to have us with them, as well as our gracious hosts from the campus and the poets and musicians we had been spending most of our time with during our stay. The stakes for any sort of dangerous conflict were pretty low; as Danticat (2010) wrote, we were not under any threat of violence in this environment (18). What was at stake, however, was the relevance and urgency of our performance content: we were there to challenge stereotypes and racism, power, and privilege, and to investigate new ways of being. As a group, Collective Energy had been utterly compelled to include every piece of poetry and song that composed our show when we were in the states. Our hosts and fellow artists were already convinced of the transformative power of art. So why, in this tranquil setting among people of so many diverse backgrounds, did I feel as if we were completely out of our league? What was on the line for Collective Energy and for me, personally, in this show? Where was the uncertainty coming from that made my palms sweat when the student artists expressed overwhelming excitement and gratitude for this opportunity? Why did I feel unsatisfied? To respond to these, my own internal reflections during this time, I turn to feminist activists and artists based in South Africa who aggressively pursue social justice in many realms of life. Essof and Wesso (2011) recommend we consider

> art as a tool that can be a medium to spread or disseminate analysis, and re-member the process of dreaming and hope for a different world, a world where many worlds fit. The re-dreaming is also a challenge to ourselves to ask the difficult questions of what next. (xxv)

In this quote, I find a line of inquiry that points to the cause for my uneasiness; in particular, the final question of "what next" echoes through that nervous tension I was feeling. The challenge for me at this time was twofold, and I didn't fully process what was happening until the whirlwind of travel was long over. First, there is the unceasing pressure of constantly asking where we are going to expand, elaborate, and pursue our commitment to social change. The need to grow and progress and change is pervasive in the socially responsible artist. The second area of tension is a question of boundaries. I've never done well with those. Collective Energy's performances in St. Augustine raised questions of space and performance as well as the persistent hope of creating "a world where many worlds fit." What happens if that mission of a different world fails? What do we do when the world I dream of is in direct opposition to the one that the audience may desire?

One characteristic unique to spoken word poetry performance is demonstrated in the defiance of the boundaries typically laid by the accoutrement of stage, seats, walls, and sound equipment. These spoken word performances are taking place out in the public domain, minus the trappings of a traditional performance setting, thus bringing the fluidity already present in a spoken word performance to the forefront in its encounter with the audience. Both the artist and the audience are at an increased risk for contact when the play is taken "out of bounds." The reason for this is that although the spectators' inactive role as explained by Laura Mulvey (1975) is already an illusion, spoken word poetry outside of a traditional performance environment goes even further to reveal the audience members' active participation in the construction of a performance. When this boundary is trespassed, there is little protocol in place for how an audience member is meant to behave and/or interact with the artist. The only consistency that remains, and is in fact emphasized after the passing of this boundary, is that the relationship—now even more viscerally obvious to all those participating in a performance event—forms the axis on which the performance rotates (Thiong'o 1997, 12). Spoken word poetry performance, particularly as performed in settings such as rural villages or by outsiders to and for a specific community, that is taken to the street so to speak, expands the potential for social change beyond the performance arena. By rubbing against existing boundaries of other, more established performance spaces that are functioning as a society's educational system, government, religious institutions, or arenas for socializing, such performances create the energy for changes. The operation of those institutions contests the limits of what is possible and acceptable interaction and point out injustices that occur within those realms as well. For this reason, spoken word poetry performance can be seen as posing a threat, and therefore situating the artist and audience member in direct danger. Structures of power dislike being questioned and don't historically respond well to being infiltrated by insurgents who interrogate the systems maintaining privilege and excluding or oppressing the masses.

Spoken word poetry performance operates as a confrontation on multiple levels. After our afternoon workshop with the instructors for the Arts in Action master's of education program at the St. Augustine campus of the University of West Indies, it became clear to me that these performances were effective forms of communication. These methods that were so similar to Boal's theater techniques combined spoken word with improvisational theater and had become integral not only to propose solutions but to create a space that was approved by the community to speak about these kinds of issues. The subjects ranged from HIV/AIDs and sexual health, which was taboo to discuss to begin with, to safe vehicle driving in the rural neighborhoods. Through community-based interventions such as these—which are incredibly interactive and seemed to be eagerly engaged in by members of the community not associated with the campus—performance works to confront, to face pervasive social issues of health and wellness, and to engage with daunting systems of injustices. Performance made room for collaborative action and agreement that did not exist without these shows. Essof and Wesso (2011) have this to say about the space that art creates:

> Art can act as a space of encounter, where the meaning(s) of piece(s) are constantly being reproduced by the audience, regenerating and revealing histories/herstories, sharing struggles, and proposing questions to think differently about how we relate to ourselves and our community. (xxv)

Indeed, Thiong'o agrees that real theater lay "where the majority of the people reside" and functions in a way that "speaks to their immediate presence" using the past to help face tomorrow" (1997, 20). Many of the outcomes of this performance project sponsored by UWI's program offered results: major shifts involving large numbers of the working-class community from illiterate to literate, more powerful political agents. Performance of this sort that succeeds in providing a means of analysis and solution-oriented sharing among disenfranchised and all too often disregarded members of the population is in large part the appeal and practicality of spoken word poetry. The reason spoken word poetry can function and adapt so easily across difference is because it is mobile: the performance comes to where the people are living daily life, delivering to their doorstep the opportunity to create a different kind of future. Rather than expecting the masses who are exhausted, busy, and without extra funds to take public transportation or pay for tickets or to attend a formal theater, spoken word poetry travels to them. And not just for a display or showcase—this performance demands the involvement of the community. Community members are transformed into actors, agents, and coproducers during spoken word poetry performance. While they may be no more able to read or write text, they will be able to remember how they were represented.

It's not just what you say; it's what you do, the stories your body tells, your silence your movements. It's the clothes you wear, the hairstyle you choose, the way you walk. Because the people are both the source of the content and the author of the finished product, when they accept the invitation to participate in a spoken word poetry performance along with the artist, they become complicit in the outcomes of a show. In other words, accountability is shared and responsibility is taken up for what takes place next. Also, since the formal borders and boundaries of performance are pushed and manipulated to fit around the performance event, and because spoken word poetry performances meet the people where they already are, changing and adjusting decisions as a result of a performance is not hard to do. Such changes have been rehearsed in the performance event, so the courage to make positive changes and decisions is less difficult to transition in daily life. Commitments agreed upon during a spoken word poetry event recur in real life because they have been rehearsed already during the performance event. By reshaping private or individual experience through a public forum, we are at the same time altering the social conditions that frame those experiences (Ellsworth 2005). Spoken word poetry that transports into communities without the limits of a theater building or venue that is used to hosting open mic performances also interrupts the routine of daily life for the community that inhabits those spaces, disturbing the ebb and flow of business as usual. This interruption and the performances that result also situate culture and cultural production within the boundaries of everyday life, inviting new readings and responses to those daily actions. Spoken word poetry performance has the ability to bring to the forefront the underground and behind-the-scenes "culture of survival" that undergirds the interactions that occur in global communities. Bringing these moments of crisis as well as joy into the forefront and exposing them through performance creates opportunities to address and relieve the tension of silence and denial that is taken up in an effort to buffer friction between discourses. Spoken word poetry performance in the context of a community is a performance that works at "refiguring ways of knowing" about identity, subjectivity, and power relations from the mouths of the audience themselves and demands a reconciliation between self and society, the inside and the outside (Ellsworth 2005, 41). Across transnational contexts, the artist's body is the site of the racialized, sexualized, and nationalized narratives during any act of performance art. Because of the autobiographical foundation of most spoken word poetry, the inside that meets the outside demands an equal amount of attention be paid to the effect of the body on the external environment it is performing in. This mutual relationship is at once assured in its effectiveness and demands of us an extreme leap of faith. This is the risk that is underwritten in spoken word poetry performance. Western artists who enter into local contexts from the outside have a responsibility to come to terms with their privilege if they wish to effectively collaborate in a global setting. Performance disarms us, makes the artist vulnerable by exposing the personal convictions and memories of their personal history to an uncontrollable end. The stories shared remove both the pain and protection of isolated experience. To take this step, to perform spoken word is to reach out, to seek connection and to invite criticisms and critical examination not only of tenderness but of superiority. Spoken word poetry is a means to say what we really believe about our lives and not just what we have been programmed to repeat; through collective construction of meaning during performances we have the opportunity to produce collective solutions (Benson and Essof 2011, 220).

It is the question of "what next" that continues to motivate the artist, the inquiry that unrelentingly buzzes in my sternum, thus it is the question I leave you with. Performing spoken word poetry insists on confrontation and collaboration, sometimes with others or with a system, and sometimes with our own dreams and desires. Dreaming, hope, and imagination: the palimpsests of performance, each time they are shared, another layer is erased and another layer written. The palimpsests are now waiting on you. Are you ready to join the cypher? What will you write? How will you perform? What do you have to contribute?

And so, it begins.

. . . you are the ultimate editor—leaving in the background noise so that I never forget where I'm recording from
But you allow me as many takes as I need to catch the right beat, make sure my chorus hits with that bass and drum
More importantly, you stay in the studio with me until it's all done.
And since I'm a perfectionist when it comes to my art, that tends to be a long time.
You've got eyes that can see in the dark, you saw your way to my heart
And you navigate us safely home sometimes right at the crack of dawn, and you still let me fall asleep in the car.

When I kept returning to the same dead end, to the same brick wall,
you offered to help me chip it away
sacrifice pours from your pores like sweat
you force me to dance
on the nights I don't feel like it
and even when my unfaithfulness stinks like the dead bodies I've tried to hide underneath
the floorboards
you record the celebrations but never seem to keep score
you helped me train myself to sing
yes, you tell me the truth but graciously allow me to forget
that only means that I keep winning
constantly
so even when my throat has been slit
if I squeeze my eyes shut
a thousand butterflies brush my tears with their wings
I can hear the chorus of two hundred parakeets sing
And it makes me keep going.
Or at least helps me to not lose my place.
You revived my faith

You are a surgeon
Steady of hand and strong of spirit

The sight of blood and tears is nothing new
Your technique is smooth and honest
You can discern between difficulty and pain, and you require that all those around you do the same
There is no room for denial
You are steady and your actions articulate
Your honey words comfort when joys seem so few and no one remembers to thank you
No one shows the gratitude that is overdue
Yet when the chips are down, we all turn to you
You have the skill to tell the truth to the family that is anxiously trying to preoccupy themselves in the waiting room
You wound and at the same time have the power to soothe
I don't know how you do it.

Each time I responded out of the pain of my past
Each time I disappointed you because my cocoon refused to crack
You never missed a beat
The strength you keep on reserve is far deeper than the impact that occurs when I speak
I observe, how could one so young know so much
It is your wisdom that I share with eager ears
It is your heart that reminds me love and fear cannot scientifically coexist in the same location

You are the teacher
You are the lover
You are the light
And this is the very best thing that I have to give you
But even these letters and words can't fit your heart in their curve
If I am Harriet Tubman then you are my rifle,
my preacher
You are where the poet goes when she needs a good word,
when she needs someone to speak to her
when the warrior that appears so brave needed a place to go when she's afraid
those pretty eyes, those steady hands, that fluorescent light, and three-way mirror,
you prop me back up, you surgery on my tumor, you don't tell me not to cry, you just give me waterproof mascara

and when I have exhausted you and when you don't think I remember
and when I called you on that warm night in September desperate to be forgiven
and now, at this moment, when I have been stripped of everything I ever thought I had
you are here
you give me back my very best thing
you tell me to go forward because like Harriet Tubman's rifle you would shoot me your self before you let me turn back and
somewhere
in the comfort of your smile
in the harsh brightness of your truth telling
when I was striking matches at the foot of our bridge
so carefully constructed
you stilled my hand
you teach me because you show me
you comb through my contradictions
careful to arrange them in style
when I was in a place only a mother could love, you didn't leave me.
when I couldn't recognize myself even in the light of your fluorescent bulb and three-way mirror
You called me by my name.

You are the quilter,
Taking my scraps, the weeping and the laughs
Taking colors and patterns anyone else would call mismatched
And you patiently, graciously
Stitch them together
You don't leave out my worst moments, my poorly chosen materials,
You just find a way to make them fit
You remind me that there is room at the altar still.

Appendix

Ashe, Ashe, Amen

A Note on Format

Poetry and scriptwriting are often implemented as ways to present research in a text in order to provoke a strong sense of empathy in an audience member or reader, specifically when such a work is based on lived experiences (Ensler 2001; Richardson 1994, 2000, 2002; Smith 1993). Poetry and performance are the specific forms of arts-based research that I focus on in this study. However, in order to best present those art forms, I call upon the use of fictionalized autoethnography, lyrics and poetry, and the format of a script throughout this text. Peggy Phelan (1993) notes that "representation always conveys more than it intends; and it is never totalizing" (2). I have no misguided hopes of fully representing the experience of Collective Energy or even my own experience, but, I dare to hope that through the transgression of combining portions of all of these formats, this research will invite multiple readings and, more importantly, multiple resistances of this interpretation will be welcomed. Just like the palimpsest offers layer upon layer of writings and histories, multiple authors and readings, our Collective Energy experience is a performance unto itself. What I offer here are several possible entryways and threads to begin tracing in this multidimensional and evolving entity. By experimenting with a variety of texts, I am asking the reader to participate in a variety of performances that are fluid so that there is a greater chance of engaging them emotionally and empathetically within the discourses that are represented here; I am asking them to relive certain events emotionally, along with me (Richardson 2000, 931). Just as I often implement techniques outlined by Boal (1979) in the *Theatre of the Oppressed* in order to rearrange students and allow them to experiment with realigning where they think they stand, I intentionally shuffle this text into a format that does not necessarily situate the reader into a linear position of control. The illusion of control and power is a barrier I have been forced to confront time and again throughout Collective Energy. Presenting our story to you in such a fashion would be a disservice and dishonest on my behalf.

As author I have control over what is included in the stories that I share, but as the storyteller, as the poet-performer, I present a fluid repetition, a version that is tinted with my own emphases and memory.

I wish to organize this representation of my research and the people involved in such a way that demands the coperformance of the reader and that also presents the text itself as a part of the performance. Live performances are full of "inconsistencies, ambiguities, ambivalence, and foreground the fact that there will always be 'unspoken themes' that cannot or will not be interrogated" (Orner, Miller, and Ellsworth 1996, 74). In other words, this text is structured intentionally to break any illusion of linear simplistic relations through the juxtaposition of multimodal performance into a single text that challenges traditional boundaries. I hope to draw attention to the ways that the cacophony of stories being told within my own pages is overlapping, drowning out, and happening in moments of time that are not neat, linear cause and effect (73). Marnina Gonick (2003) addresses the complications that retelling stories provoke by suggesting that a disruptive text is one that makes room for "the representation of many different voices, as well as the many voices of a single individual" (58). Gonick goes on to correlate the consideration of voices as contingent and relational by pointing out that doing so allows for a text that acknowledges and supports the construction of identities and discourses as plural, contradictory, partial, and strategic (58). This assertion of the characteristics of voice in no way attempts to costume the cultural and social frameworks that shape the stories being told (or not told), nor do they attempt to disguise the capitalistic profits that are due to the researcher at the conclusion of any project.

Methodology

Because performance is such a physical method, and indeed is a method of inquiry in and of itself, it is incredibly difficult for me to attempt to translate from a performance text to a written text. I'm limited before I even begin. I'm asking that you understand the research that is presented here is partial and fictionalized because that is the only way I am able to reconcile myself with writing about the intense eight-month experience that was Collective Energy. This lopsided view doesn't pull evenly from each student artist's quotes or artistic contributions. In this case, retrospect does not always promise the clearest vision.

There are an increasing number of academic contributions that have been made that define, situate, and examine the usefulness of performance and art in a classroom setting, some of which provide guidelines on how to implement such techniques, as well as collections that explore connections between art and activism (Becker 1994; Boal 1979; Denizen 2003; Felshin 1995; Garoian 1999; Giroux 2006; Kester 1998; Klebesadel 2003). I have found support in most of these references and use them to frame a specific personal account of where I am and where I am not in the system of higher education and the world.

The Cast of Collective Energy

Initially, this project was developed as a cultural program for the Paul Robeson Cultural Center (PRCC) on the campus of the Pennsylvania State University. The director of the PRCC at the time, my colleague and friend Toby Jenkins (now TJ Henry, who is introduced more in-depth in the text) conceptualized this initiative as an "arts in action" program. I was a full-time graduate student and an instructor on campus when Toby hired me as a graduate assistant at the PRCC. Toby, knowing my experience as a spoken word artist, met with me to brainstorm an idea she had for a cultural program that would introduce the concept of arts as a form of social action to our broader campus. What grew from this meeting gave shape and form to a void I had been looking to fill since my arrival at our rural campus—a place where I could spit. Generally speaking, the program addressed a need felt on campus by students of all colors to have a venue for creative expression in relationship to their pressing cultural, historical, and social issues. The group of student artists I came to work with on a weekly basis named themselves Collective Energy—the title was chosen to honor the various types of skills, flavors, and personalities involved. We jokingly referred to the jingle for an old cartoon, *Captain Planet*, because the plot of the show involved several superheroes that represented different elements, but their greatest power was available to them when they converged. Collective Energy had the makings of a colorful kaleidoscope with each member contributing a different shade of experiences and strengths to the stage.

Background and Description

Collective Energy is a group designed in direct response to the growing need to develop both critical art consumers and performers in a society dominated by popular culture. The Cultural Arts in Social Action Initiative was a series of several programs developed and hosted through the Paul Robeson Cultural Center that were focused on providing students with a means to explore various elements of culture and the arts. During my time working at the PRCC, these programs included Bed: A Spoken Word Lounge, Collective Energy, and the Arts in Action Cultural Immersion Spring Break.

We created multiple performance opportunities of a wide scope in order to expose the student artists participating in Collective Energy to the broadest performance experience possible. Collective Energy served as the headliner at the regular Bed: Spoken Word Lounge on the University Park Penn State campus and also participated in travel performances to other local colleges, out-of-state high schools, correctional facilities, and other Penn State campuses. Collective Energy was also involved in hosting outside groups on our home campus, during which we conducted poetry workshops for a variety of audiences. The group creatively conversed with their collegiate peers as well as local and international communities about relevant social issues through the use of spoken word poetry, song, and music. This initiative was unlike any other that the campus had ever seen. The entire Cultural Arts in Social Action Initiative existed only due to the deep level of commitment Toby had to the mission of the PRCC and to community outreach.

Because this was the premiere of the program, I was able to handpick who was invited to join as a member of the inaugural Collective Energy team. There were two key characteristics shared by each of the student artists I invited: an explicit desire to cultivate their artistic skills and an eagerness to show those skills off. I recognized the performers who were hungry—eager to grow, ready to learn, willing to hustle. The hustle was something I could relate to, and respect. The time commitment for these student artists was going to be intense, and the work and effort required to make the programs successful required the sort of discipline that would show up early and stay late. The subject matter, the performances that compiled our "final" show, the questions we used to critique each piece, and the transitions between performances that resulted in our final hour and a half performance would be the end result of group practices, trial, and error. Early on, we agreed that learning to be critical consumers and producers of art was a desire we shared. Keeping the aspiration to grow our level of cultural analysis at the forefront of our decision-making process when it was time to select what pieces to perform forced us to examine with greater conviction what we were producing. As the name "Collective Energy" implies, one of my personal goals for this particular group was to organize our meetings so that the input and feedback of *all* of our members determined most of the artistic and social elements that would be included. As an artist, I wanted excellent performances; as a feminist pedagogue and activist, I was committed to structuring the learning experiences with my students such that the power and decision-making process was as democratic as possible. This way, even the least experienced student artist had space and opportunity to share ideas and contribute to the direction Collective Energy took artistically. I formatted an outline for the experience in the form of a syllabus; however, the workshop plans and topics were fluid and were revised by Toby and me often at the last minute as is usually necessary when implementing a cultural program for the first time.

While this was not the first cultural program I had planned, it was by far the most personal one. The reason I was chosen to become involved (indeed, part of the reason that I was hired to work at the PRCC to begin with) is because of my background in performance. I had been a spoken word artist and amateur actor for almost six years, and I have both earned a living and found fulfillment in producing resistant performances. I was a full-time student and a full-time artist—meaning I was booking paying gigs at venues across the United States and abroad—during the time period that Collective Energy first formed, and that background qualified me to assist the newer student artists in their growth and development because they had less experience performing and composing their own original work. It feels odd even now to include a qualifying statement within this text, but it needs to be clear that I did not assume a leadership position with no personal investment in the broad development and general well-being of each of the student artists involved. I entered this engagement with clear and definitive personal goals and expectations, and I was shocked when they were not met or in some cases even regarded. I had endeavored to create what Mary Louise Pratt (1999) named the "contact zone"—an area defined as "social spaces where cultures meet, clash, and grapple with each other, often in contexts of highly asymmetrical relations of power" (33). Not only had I forged ahead, I had invited students that I was responsible for to expose themselves and exchange personal details with one another, to submit to my leadership, and to then take the major risk of showcasing their often autobiographical spoken word poetry performances to a hegemonic and privileged public. I was invested in the success of the various branch programs that resulted from Collective Energy, and that success was evaluated on the reaction and response—at the very least the size—of the audience in attendance. And although performance has been central to my life for some years now, I never dared assume that I would have the opportunity to conduct and produce academic research on the subject. Because of the widespread interest and marketability of spoken word poetry, I find it even more compelling to centralize making overt connections between the abstract concept of performing cultural representations and the reality that makes up the lives of my students of color at the university. The skills to do so are crucial and relevant to their successful navigation of college life and larger society. Learning to view ourselves as legitimate cultural producers has not always been easy. Just as this text offers the scholarly analysis of spoken word poetry a new sort of validated sense of significance in a world of language and power relations, it is my hope that should any member of Collective Energy pick up this text they would see themselves respectfully represented and acknowledged in a new and different way—not simply because I said they should be, but because their own work and words make up the core of this story. I had the absolute permission of each member to record and recount everything that happened within our meetings, as well as their permission (and even request) to use their real names. The poetry and song lyrics in their entirety that are included within these pages have the authors' names listed where they are located in the text so that they receive full credit for their work. Every song lyric and poem included in this text was performed publicly at some point during the Collective Energy experience; however, most of the conversations that the analysis is structured around took place either within the company of only Collective Energy members or in one-on-one interviews that I conducted with each member.

Collective Energy met each Tuesday night for three hours at Toby's home. We ate a home-cooked meal together prior to each meeting and didn't officially begin our sessions until about 6:30 p.m. I recorded on videotape all of our group meetings, performances (which we watched in our group meetings sometimes), and, much later, the one-on-one interviews I conducted with student members. This collection of data prior to having a firm research question and clear system of analysis has made this process feel somewhat like a breeched birth—it has come out feet first. When we hatched the idea of an integrated arts performance group, my original intention was to develop a curriculum and turn the experience into a class during the spring semester so that our plans to take the students on a study abroad experience could potentially receive funding. This process was so complicated that it made more sense to keep it as an informal but very structured weekly meeting. I was mostly responsible for planning our lesson and determining what activities would take place during the weekly meetings. The local performances we participated in on Penn State's satellite campuses served as a sort of rehearsal for our "final show." They were an opportunity to experiment with different versions and choreography of our performance pieces until we arrived in Trinidad and Tobago. Our "final show" was performed at the annual Literacy Festival held on the St. Augustine campus. The international portion of the program was to serve as a culminating end-of-the-year experience for Collective Energy. There is a wellspring of data rich with stories from the international experience we shared, and I turn to those outcomes and the further questions the international experience invites in the final chapter; however, I focus this story on what took place prior to our trip. It is the process, after all, that truly tells the tale of the performance. The rehearsal and revision process often reveals not only what we learn and choose to present to an audience in a "final product" but *how* and *why* we learn and teach one another. Paying close attention to the process invites a feminist approach to reflexivity and a valued tradition of action-oriented outcomes. Most of this text comes from exchanges that occurred in the midst of fleshing out the year of planning and performing that occurred because of the significance that negotiating social relations bears on performance.

This new project was in addition to the regular cultural programming that I was responsible for, the classes I was teaching, and the courses I was taking. Toby and I agreed that the program should remain intimate, with only a small number of students able to participate. I relished this rare chance; I was completely aware of the privilege it was to pick and choose whom I wanted to include. Before this even became a research project, I was tangled in the web that power often weaves. What makes this even tougher to admit was that I enjoyed and certainly exercised that power. Most of the feminist teaching that I've received did not equip me well for this feeling. I had come to believe that power was a bad thing, something a feminist would never work to gain or use for her own benefit. But as Foucault (1984) reminds us, "Everything is dangerous, which is not the same as bad," and this was a danger I was eager to flirt with (343). So I invited six students plus Toby and me for a total of eight participants, all of whom I had worked with in some capacity before. Everyone I invited accepted and agreed to participate. Here I offer a brief, random sample of details that mark each of these student artists on a map of sorts to provide an outline of my motives for choosing them. The cast list for Collective Energy is as follows:

Tony

Originally from Washington, D.C./Maryland, Tony was a second-year grad student at Penn State. A young Black man, first-generation college student, and fairly new to Penn State, Tony struggled with themes of responsibility often because so many young folks looked up to him. He had worked for some time prior to his decision to attend graduate school and major in college student affairs. His desk was literally attached to my desk in the PRCC, and we worked and played hard together. He already had some experience performing his poetry prior to joining Collective Energy. We had traveled to Tanzania as part of a women's studies study-abroad course together the summer before as well.

Q'tyashia

Also known simply as "Q," this vibrant young lady remains one of the hardest-working people I know. She hails from the island of Antigua, and when she is angry or speaking very quickly her accent comes thick and fast. She has always held two jobs and was president of our Caribbean Student Association during the first year of Collective Energy. She also had a triple major and took her first women's studies class with me as the instructor. Her work ethic makes Q stand out. She was probably the youngest poet in the group in terms of both age and experience writing and sharing her poetry.

Carlos

By far the most prolific writer of the group, Carlos was always teased by us about his notebook because of the loose-leaf pages he was forced to add and the tiny size of his print. Hailing from Philly, Carlos is Puerto Rican and Black. He studies Kung Fu and is very conscious of his health and his way of life. Carlos was not technically enrolled in school during Collective Energy. Carlos is also a dancer—break dance, salsa, hip hop, you name it. We call him "Shooter" sometimes because of one of his poems. He boarded an airplane for the first time when we left the country for Trinidad and Tobago.

Stacey

A dreamer, an eclectic artist, and a huge Saul Williams fan, Stacey and I first met on the set of a theater production of *The Colored Museum* that we were both cast in. I was present at her first open mic performance, and I was the person she texted when she competed in (and won) her first slam. Stacey has been in attendance at most of the open mics the PRCC has sponsored. She is based out of Philadelphia and was a junior. Stacey is a gymnast and a dancer and loves Jill Scott.

Jonathan

Because of his slim build, old-school dance moves, and smooth voice, we nicknamed Jonathan "Ol' Silky." With a mother who is a college music professor, Jonathan comes from a family of singers and musicians. An aspiring pianist and guitar player, this Black and Puerto Rican soul singer joined Collective Energy during his first year of graduate school at Penn State. After attending a Historically Black College for his undergrad degree, where he was heavily involved on campus as a student leader, Penn State was a complicated adjustment. Jonathan was also a college student affairs major.

Alyssa

We called Alyssa our Songbird because of her deep voice and the harmonies that she belts out. One of a kind in her styles both on and off the stage, Alyssa was on the trip to Tanzania that Tony and I were a part of the summer prior to the formation of Collective Energy. She was my director for a production of *The Vagina Monologues*, and she also participated in an a cappella group on campus. A fervent photographer, Alyssa has also been dancing since she was a child. Her red hair and freckles mark Alyssa as the only White participant in Collective Energy. Her contributions artistically and thoughtfully make her shine.

Toby

Every thoughtful and provoking poem that Toby has shared within our group and on stage has earned her the name "The Teacher." As director of the cultural center, Toby exudes confidence and has a reputation and expectations for excellence in all aspects of life. She is in a constant state of internal critical reflection that often adds another layer of intensity to her work as an artist and a professional. She was earning her PhD during the time Collective Energy took place. I have known Toby for almost as long as I've been at Penn State, and she is more than a boss, a mentor, and a role model; she is a friend.

Crystal

My name is Crystal Leigh. I'm originally from Louisiana and I grew up in Virginia Beach. I have a background in theater and have been performing spoken word poetry at different venues around the country and beyond since I was twenty-one years old. I have produced two CDs of my own. I try to avoid specifically naming my ethnicity and often outright refuse to answer questions about my background—if I must be categorized, I prefer to subscribe to a "mixed" group. At the same time, I name the racial categories that the other student artists belong to, which may appear unfair. I realize that as author of this story I wield this power, and I acknowledge that. I do this because each of the students named the ways in which they culturally identified and often spoke of the influence those subjectivities had on their performances. My subjectivity and racially mixed body also dictates a great deal of my performance, and therefore I name myself as mixed. This is an issue that threads throughout this story, so for now I set it back down.

In reference to one of my poems and because of the passionate nature of my performance style, the other members of Collective Energy sometimes call me That Fire.

References

Adichie, C. N. 2007. *Half of a Yellow Sun.* Harpswell, ME: Penguin.

Alcoff, L. 1995. "The Problem of Speaking for Others." *Who Can Speak? Authority and Critical Identity.* Ed. J. Roof. Chicago, IL: University Illinois Press. 97–119.

Alsultany, E. 2002. "Los Intersticios: Recasting Moving Selves." *This Bridge We Call Home: Radical Visions for Transformation.* Ed. G. Anzaldúa and A. L. Keating. New York, NY: Routledge. 106–109.

Althusser, L. 1971. "Ideology and Ideological State Appartuses (Notes Towards an Investigation)." *Lenin and Philosophy and Other Essays.* Trans. B. Brewster. New York, NY: Monthly Review Press. 127–186.

Anzaldúa, G. 1981. "Speaking in Tongues: A Letter to Third World Women Writers." *This Bridge Called My Back: Writings by Radical Women of Color.* Ed. C. Moraga and G. Anzaldúa. Watertown, NY: Persephone. 165–174.

Anzaldúa, G., A. and Keating, eds. 2002. *This Bridge We Call Home: Radical Visions for Transformation.* New York, NY: Routledge.

Baldwin, J. 1969. "Sweet Lorraine." *To Be Young Gifted and Black: Lorraine Hansberry in Her Own Words.* Adapted by R. Nemiroff. New York, NY: Random House. xvii–xx.

Becker, C., ed. 1994. *The Subversive Imagination: Artists, Society, and Social Responsibility.* New York, NY: Routledge.

———. 2001. *Surpassing the Spectacle: Global Transformations and the Changing Politics of Art.* New York, NY: Rowman & Littlefield.

Bell, S., M. Morrow, and E. Tastsoglou. 1999. "Teaching in Environments of Resistance." *Meeting the Challenge: Innovative Feminist Pedagogies in Action.* Ed. M. Mayberry and E. Rose. New York, NY: Routledge. 23–42.

Benson, K., and S. Essof. 2011. "Out of the Pages of This Volume." *My Dream Is to Be Bold: Our Work to End Patriarchy.* Ed. S. Essof and R. Wesso. Cape Town, SA: Pambazuka Press. 227–246.

Boal, A. 1979. *Theatre of the Oppressed.* New York, NY: Urizen Books.

Bologh, R. 1984. "Feminist Social Theorizing and Moral Reasoning: On Difference and Dialectic." *Sociological Theory 1984.* Ed. American Sociological Association. San Francisco, CA: Jossey-Bass. 373–393.

Bost, S. 2001. " 'Be Deceived If Ya Wanna Be Foolish': (Re)constructing the Body, Genre, and Gender in Feminist Rap." *Postmodern Culture* 12: 1.

Brennan, J., A. Burton, and Y. Lawi. 2007. *Dar es Salaam: Histories from an Emerging African Metropolis.* Dar es Salaam, TZ: Mkuki Na Nyota.

Bristow, A., and J. Esper. 1988. "A Feminist Research Ethos." *A Feminist Ethic for Social Science Research.* Ed. Nebraska Sociological Feminist Collective. Lewistown, NY: Edwin Mellen Press. 80–88.

Brookes, A. L. 1992. *Feminist Pedagogy: An Autobiographical Approach.* Halifax, NS: Fernwood.

Browdy de Hernandez, J., P. Dongala, O. Jolaosho, and A. Serafin. 2010 *African Women Writing Resistance: Contemporary Voices.* Madison, WI: U of Wisconsin P.

Brown, R. N., and C. J. Kwakye, eds. 2012. *Wish to Live: The Hip-Hop Feminism Pedagogy Reader.* Educational Psychology. Volume 3. New York, NY: Peter Lang.

Butler, J. 1993. *Bodies That Matter: On the Discursive Limits of Sex.* New York, NY: Routledge.

Bynoe, Y. 2004. *Stand and Deliver: Political Activism, Leadership, and Hip Hop Culture.* Brooklyn, NY: Soft Skull Press.

Carson, T., and D. Sumara, eds. 1997. *Action Research as a Living Practice.* New York, NY: Peter Lang.

Chang, J. 2005. *Can't Stop Won't Stop: A History of the Hip-Hop Generation.* London, England: St. Martin's.

Christians, C. 2000. "Ethics and Politics in Qualitative Research." In *Handbook of Qualitative Research*, 2nd ed. Ed. N. K. Denzin and Y. S. Lincoln. Thousand Oaks, CA: Sage. 133–135.

Collins, B, ed. 2003. *Poetry 180: A Turning Back to Poetry.* New York, NY: Random House Trade.

Collins, P. H. 1991. *Black Feminist Thought: Knowledge, Consciousness, and the Politics of Empowerment.* New York, NY: Routledge.

———. 1999. "Mammies, Matriarchs, and Other Controlling Images." *Feminist Philosophies.* Ed. J. Kournay, J. Sterba, and R. Tong. Upper Saddle River, NJ: Prentice Hall. 142–152.

———. 2006. *From Black Power to Hip Hop: Racism, Nationalism, and Feminism.* Philadelphia, PA: Temple UP.

Crenshaw, K. 1989. "Demarginalizing the Intersection of Race and Sex: A Black Feminist Critique of Antidiscrimination Doctrine, Feminist Theory, and Antiracist Politics." *The University of Chicago Legal Forum* 140: 139–167.

Danticat, E. 2010. *Create Dangerously: The Immigrant Artist at Work.* Princeton, NJ: Princeton UP.

———. 1990. *Breath Eyes Memory.* New York, NY: Random House.

———. 1996. *Krik? Krak!* New York, NY: Knopf Doubleday.

Davies, B. 2000. "Eclipsing the Constitutive Power of Discourse: The Writing of Janette Turner Hospital." *Working the Ruins: Feminist Poststructural Theory and Methods in Education.* Ed. E. St. Pierre and W. Pillow. New York: Routledge. 179–198.

Dehli, K. 1991. "Leaving the Comfort of Home: Working through Feminisms." *Unsettling Relations: The University as a Site of Feminist Struggles.* Toronto: Women's Press. 45–65.

Denzin, N. K. 2003. *Performance Ethnography: Critical Pedagogy and the Politics of Culture.* Thousand Oaks, CA: Sage.

Drake, J. 2002. "Variations on Negation: Breaking the Frame with Lorna Simpson and Adrian Piper." *Interfaces: Women, Autobiography, Image, Performance.* Ann Arbor: U of Michigan P. 211–239.

Du Bois, W. E. B. 1903. *The Souls of Black Folk: Essays and Sketches.* Chicago, IL: A. C. McClurg.

Dyson, M. E. 1996. *Holler If You Hear Me.* New York, NY: Basic Civitas.

———. 2011. *Can You Hear Me Now? The Inspiration, Wisdom, and Insight of Michael Eric Dyson.* New York, NY: Basic Civitas.

Eleveld, M., ed. 2003. *The Spoken Word Revolution: Slam, Hip Hop, and the Poetry of a New Generation.* Naperville, IL: Sourcebooks.

———. 2005. *The Spoken Word Revolution: Slam, Hip Hop, and the Poetry of a New Generation.* Naperville, IL: Sourcebooks MediaFusion.

Ellsworth, E. 1989. "Why Doesn't This Feel Empowering? Working through the Repressive Myths of Critical Pedagogy." *Harvard Educational Review* 59.3: 297–324.

———. 2005. *Places of Learning: Media, Architecture, Pedagogy.* New York, NY: Routledge.

Endsley, C. L. 2014. "We Do It for the People: Spoken Word Poets and Hip Hop Artists as Agents of Social Change." *See You at the Crossroads: Hip Hop Scholarship at the Intersections of Dialectical Harmony, Ethics, Aesthetics, and Panoply of Voices.* Ed. B. Porfilio, D. Roychoudhury, and L. Gardner. Rotterdam, Netherlands: Sense. 45–58.

———. 2013. "Mamma Says: Knowledge Production and Feminist Activism." *Family, Community, and Higher Education.* Ed. T. Jenkins. New York, NY: Taylor and Francis. 49–64.

———. 2012. "This Is the Re-Mix: President Obama, Racial Ambiguity, and Hip Hop." *Journal of Black Masculinities* 2.2, 39–52.

Ensler, E. 2001. *The Vagina Monologues.* New York, NY: Villard.

Escobar, E. 1994. "The Heuristic Power of Art." *The Subversive Imagination: Artists, Society, and Social Responsibility.* Ed. C. Becker. New York, NY: Routledge. 33–54.

Essof, S., and R. Wesso. 2011. *My Dream Is to Be Bold: Our Work to End Patriarchy.* Cape Town, SA: Pambazuka Press.

Fanon, F. 1967. *Black Skin, White Masks.* New York, NY: Grove Press.

Felman, J. L. 2001. *Never a Dull Moment: Teaching and the Art of Performance.* New York, NY: Routledge.

Felshin, N., ed. 1995. *But Is It Art? The Spirit of Art as Activism.* Seattle, WA: Bay Press.

Fine, M. 1992. *Disruptive Voices: The Possibilities of Feminist Research.* Ann Arbor, MI: U of Michigan P.

Foucault, M. 1984. *The Foucault Reader.* New York, NY: Pantheon.

Freire, P. 1972. *Pedagogy of the Oppressed.* New York, NY: Herder and Herder.

———. 2000. *Pedagogy of the Oppressed,* 30th anniversary edition. New York, NY: Bloomsbury Academic.

Freire, P., and D. P. Macedo. 1993. *Pedagogy of the City.* New York, NY: Continuum.

Garoian, C. 1999. *Performing Pedagogy: Toward an Art of Politics.* Albany, NY: State U of New York P.

George, N. 2005. *Hip Hop America.* New York, NY: Penguin.

Gilbert, K., ed. 2001. *The Emotional Nature of Qualitative Research.* Washington, DC: CRC Press.

Giroux, H. 1992. "Cultural Studies, Resisting Difference, and the Return of Critical Pedagogy." *Border Crossings.* New York, NY: Routledge.

———. 2006. *The Giroux Reader.* Boulder, CO: Paradigm.

Glen, L. N. 2008. "Lyric Inquiry." *Handbook of the Arts in Qualitative Research: Perspecitves, Methodologies, Examples, and Issues.* Eds. J. G. Knowles and A. L. Cole. Thousand Oaks, CA: Sage. 93–102.

Gómez-Peña, G., and R. Sifuentes. 2011. *Exercises for Rebel Artists: Radical Performance Pedagogy.* New York, NY: Routledge.

Gonick, M. 2003. *Between Femininities: Ambivalence, Identity, and the Education of Girls.* Albany, NY: State U of New York P.

Grumet, M. 1988. *Bitter Milk: Women and Teaching.* Amherst, MA: U of Massachusetts P.

———. 1997. *Education: Discipline Analysis.* Baltimore, MD: National Center for Curriculum Transformation Resources on Women.

Hansberry, L. 1971. *To Be Young, Gifted and Black: Lorraine Hansberry in Her Own Words.* Adapted by R. Nemiroff. New York, NY: Random House.

Harper, H. 2000. *Wild Words, Dangerous Desires: High school girls and Feminist Avant-Garde Writing.* New York, NY: Peter Lang.

hooks, b. 1989. *Talking Back: Thinking Feminist, Thinking Black.* Boston, MA: South End Press.

———. 1993. *Sisters of the Yam: Black Women and Self-Recovery.* Boston, MA: South End Press.

———. 1994. *Teaching to Transgress: Education as the Practice of Freedom.* New York, NY: Routledge.

———. 2000. *All About Love: New Visions.* New York, NY: Perennial.

———. 2001. *Salvation.* New York, NY: HarperCollins.

———. 2002. *Communion: The Female Search for Love.* New York, NY: HarperCollins.

Irwin, R., and S. Springgay. 2008. "A/r/tography as Practice-Based Research." *Arts-Based Research in Education: Foundations for Practice.* Ed. M. Cahnmann-Taylor and R. Siegesmund. New York, NY: Routledge. 103–124.

———. 2008. "A/r/tography as Practice-Based Research." *Being with A/r/tography.* Ed. S. Springgay, R. Irwin, C. Leggo, and P. Gouzouasis. Rotterdam, Netherlands: Sense. xix–1.

Jagger, A. 1992. "Feminist Ethics." *Encyclopedia of Ethics.* Ed. L. Becker and C. Becker. New York, NY: Garland Press.

Jocson, K. 2005. "'Taking it to the mic': Pedagogy of June Jordan's Poetry for the People and Partnership with an Urban High School." *English Education* (January): 132–148.

Jordan, J. 1995. Introduction. *June Jordan's Poetry for the People: A Revolutionary Blueprint.* New York, NY: Routledge. 1–12.

Kester, G., ed. 1998. *Art, Activism, and Oppositionality.* Durham, NC: Duke UP.

Kitwana, B. 2002. *The Hip Hop Generation: Young Blacks and the Crisis in African American Culture.* New York, NY: Basic Books.

———. 2004. "The Challenge of Rap Music from Cultural Movement to Political Power." *That's the Joint! The Hip-Hop Studies Reader.* Ed. M. A. Neal and M. Forman. New York, NY: Routledge. 341–350.

Klebesadel, H. 2003. "Feminist Activist Art in Action." *Newsletter of Wisconsin Women's Network.* http://www.wiwomensnetwork.org/activistart.html. Accessed 20 June 2006.

KRS One. 2002. *Temple of Hip Hop.* Koch Records.

Kula, M. 2002. "When Feminism Goes Pop!" *Bitch* (Spring): 54–59.

Kuryluk, E. 1994. "A Plea for Irresponsibility." *The Subversive Imagination: Artists, Society, and Social Responsibility.* Ed. C. Becker. New York, NY: Routledge.13–20.

Langellier, K. M. 1998. "Voiceless Bodies, Bodiless Voices: The Future of Personal Narrative Performance." *The Future of Performance Studies: Visions and Revisions.* Washington, DC: National Communication Association. 207–213.

Lather, P. 1988. "Feminist Perspectives on Empowering Research Methodologies." *Women's Studies International Forum* 11.6: 569–581.

Low, B. 2011. *Slam School: Learning Through Conflict in the Hip-Hop and Spoken Word Classroom.* Stanford, CA: Stanford UP.

Luttrell, W. 1997. *Schoolsmart and Motherwise: Working-Class Women's Identity and Schooling.* New York, NY: Routledge.

Magubane, Z. 2006. "Globalization and Gangers Rap: Hip Hop in the Post-Apartheid City." *The Vinyl Ain't Final: Hip Hop and the Globalization of Black Popular Culture.* Ed. D. Basu and S. J. Lemelle. Ann Arbor, MI: Pluto Press. 208–229.

Martin, C., ed. 1996. "Bearing Witness: Anna Deavere Smith from Community to Theatre to Mass Media." *A Sourcebook of Feminist Theatre and Performance: On and Beyond the Stage.* New York, NY: Routledge. 81–93.

Matthews, A. 2005. *A Panther in Africa.* DVD.

Mohanty, C. 2003. *Feminism Without Borders: Decolonizing Theory, Practicing Solidarity.* Durham, NC: Duke UP.

Moraga, C. 1981. "La Guera." *This Bridge Called My Back: Writings by Radical Women of Color.* Ed. C. Moraga and G. Anzaldúa. Watertown, NY: Persephone. 27–34.

Morgan, J. 2000. *When Chickenheads Come Home to Roost: A Hip-Hop Feminist Breaks It Down.* New York, NY: Simon and Schuster.

Muller, L. 1985. *June Jordan's Poetry for the People: A Revolutionary Blueprint.* New York, NY: Routledge.

Mulvey, L. 1975. "Visual Pleasure and Narrative Cinema." *Screen* 16.3 (Autumn): 6–18.

Neal, M. A., and M. Forman. 2011. *That's the Joint! The Hip Hop Studies Reader.* New York, NY: Routledge.

Noddings, N. 1984. *Caring: A Feminine Approach to Ethics and Moral Education.* Berkeley, CA: U of California P.

Ntarangwi, M. 2009. *East African Hip Hop: Youth Culture and Globalization.* Urbana-Champaign, IL: U of Illinois P.

Orner, M. 1992. "Interrupting the Calls for Student Voice in 'Liberatory' Education: A Feminist Poststructuralist Perspective." *Feminisms and Critical Pedagogy.* Ed. C. Luke and J. Gore. New York: Routledge. 74–89.

Orner, M., J. Miller, and E. Ellsworth. 1996. "Excessive Moments and Educational Discourses That Try to Contain Them." *Educational Theory* 46: 73–91.

Phelan, P. 1993. *Unmarked: The Politics of Performance.* New York, NY: Routledge.

Porfilio, B., and P. Carr. 2010. *Youth Culture, Education, and Resistance: Subverting the Commercial Ordering of Life.* Rotterdam, Netherlands: Sense.

Porfilio, B., and M. Viola, eds. 2012. *Hip Hop(e): The Cultural Practice and Critical Pedagogy of International Hip-Hop.* New York, NY: Peter Lang.

Pough, G. 2007. *Home Girls Make Some Noise: Hip Hop Feminism Anthology.* Upper Saddle River, NJ: Parker.

———. 2007. *Home Girls Make Some Noise: Hip Hop Feminism Anthology.* Upper Saddle River, NJ: Parker.

Pratt, M. L. 1999. "Arts of the Contact Zone." *Ways of Reading 5th Edition.* Ed. D. Bartholomae and A. Petrosky. New York, NY: Bedford/St. Martin's. 33–40.

Pratt, M. L., and K. E. Newman, eds. 1999. *Critical Passions: Selected Essays.* Durham, NC: Duke UP.

Ramazanoglu, C., and J. Holland. 2002. *Feminist Methodology: Challenges and Choices.* Thousand Oaks, CA: Sage.

Reinharz, S. 1992. *Feminist Methods in Social Research.* New York, NY: Oxford UP.

Richardson, E. 2006. *Hip Hop Literacies.* New York, NY: Routledge.

Richardson, L. 1994. "Nine Poems." *Journal of Contemporary Ethnography* 23: 3–13.

———. 2002. "Poetic Representation of Interviews." *Handbook of Interview Research: Context and Method.* Ed. J. F. Gubrium and J. A. Holstein. Thousand Oaks, CA: Sage. 887–891.

———. 2000. "Skirting a Pleated Text: De-Disciplining an Academic Life." *Working the Ruins: Feminist Poststructural Theory and Methods in Education.* New York, NY: Routledge. 153–163.

Rockhill, K. 1987. "Literacy as Threat and Desire: Longing to be SOMEBODY." *Women in Education: A Canadian Perspective.* Calgary: Detselig Enterprises. 315–331.

Rose, T. 1994. *Black Noise: Rap Music and Black Culture in Contemporary America.* Boston, MA: Wesleyan.

Russell Simmons' Def Poetry Jam. Perf. S. Lathan, D. Hoch, R. Simmons, J. C. Moore, M. Def. HBO Studios. 2004. DVD.

Saucier, P. K. 2011. *Native Tongues: An African Hip-Hop Reader.* Lawrenceville, NJ: Africa World Press.

Shannon, P., ed. 2001. *Becoming Political, Too: New Readings and Writings on the Politics of Literacy Education.* Portsmouth, NH: Heinemann.

Simon, R. 1992. *Teaching against the Grain: Texts for a Pedagogy of Possibility.* New York, NY: Bergen and Garvey.

Smith, A. D. 1993. *Fires in the Mirror: Crown Heights, Brooklyn, and Other Identities.* Garden City, NY: Anchor.

Smith, L. T. 1999. *Decolonizing Methodologies: Research and Indigenous Peoples.* London: Zed Books.

Smith, S., and J. Watson, eds. 2002. *Interfaces: Women, Autobiography, Image, Performance.* Ann Arbor, MI: U of Michigan P.

Smith, V. 2001. "Class and Gender in Narratives of Passing." *Feminist Consequences: Theory for the New Century.* West Sussex, NY: Columbia UP. 189–212.

Springgay, S. 2008. "An Ethics of Embodiment." *Being with A/r/tography.* Ed. S. Springgay, R. Irwin, C. Leggo, and P. Gouzouasis. Rotterdam, Netherlands: Sense. 153–166.

St. Pierre, E. 2000. Nomadic Inquiry in the Smooth Spaces of the Field: A Preface. *Working the Ruins: Feminist Poststructural Theory and Methods in Education.* Ed. E. St. Pierre and W. Pillow. New York, NY: Routledge. 258–276.

Thiong'o, N. 1986. *Decolonizing the Mind: The Politics of Language in African Literature.* London, England: James Currey.

———. 1997. "Enactments of Power: The Politics of Performance Space." *The Drama Review* 41: 11–30.

———. 2011. *Decolonizing the Mind: The Politics of Language in African Literature.* London, UK: Heinemann.

Underiner, T. 2000. "Beyond Recognition, Beholden: Toward a Pedagogy of Privilege." *Signs: Journal of Women and Culture in Society* 25: 4. 1293–1298.

Unger, R. K. 1981. "Sex as Social Reality: Field and Laboratory Research." *Psychology of Women Quarterly* 5: 645–653.

Walkerdine, V. 1990. *Schoolgirl Fictions.* Brooklyn, NY: Verso Books.

Weedon, C. 1997. *Feminist Practice and Poststructuralist Theory.* Malden, MA: Blackwell.

Winnicott, D. W. 1989. *Playing and Reality.* New York, NY: Routledge.

Index